W9-BYO-736

THE PASTOR'S MANUAL

THE
PASTOR'S MANUAL

JAMES RANDOLPH HOBBS, D.D., L.L.D.

BROADMAN PRESS
NASHVILLE, TENNESSEE

Printed in the United States of America

*This volume
is affectionately dedicated
to*

W. A. McComb, D.D.,

*my father in the
ministry*

CONTENTS

CONTENTS—Continued

Preface

In offering this little book to the ministry, the author entertains hope that it may be found useful.

The work of the modern minister is multifarious and exacting. Therefore, it is to be supposed that anything that will contribute to his success and the better performance of his many duties should receive a warm welcome.

The author of this book is a pastor of some twenty years' experience, which experience embraces every manner of pastorate, from the small country one to that of a large city church. The suggestions in this little book relating to how to perform the various tasks of a pastor are the outgrowth of this varied experience.

The author does not claim that this work is perfect, but believes that it may prove helpful and suggestive to all pastors, especially the young brethren just entering upon pastoral work.

The author was encouraged to undertake the preparation of this little volume by Dr.

W. B. Crumpton, the Nestor of Alabama Baptists, who obliged him by making many kind suggestions.

Many other brethren have offered valuable suggestions which have been materially helpful in preparing this book. Special mention should be accorded Dr. Geo. W. McDaniel, Dr. I. J. Van Ness, Dr. J. J. Taylor and Rev. D. M. Gardner.

Having decided to bring out a new edition of The Pastor's Manual in more convenient and attractive form, the publishers suggested to the author that he might have the privilege of instituting any alterations or revisions that may seem good to him. Study of the book and its constant use over the years show that few revisions are necessary. Four or five of the poems were dropped. One of the Funeral Services seemed unnecessary, one of the Marriage Ceremonies was dropped, and that part under the head of the Church relating to organization was cut out, because church organization has come to vary and change so rapidly now and because new books suggesting newer forms of organization are obtainable from year to year. It is hoped that the new form of the new edition will give The Pastor's Manual additional popularity and a larger field of service.

JAMES RANDOLPH HOBBS

Pastor's Office,
First Baptist Church,
Birmingham, Alabama.

Notes on Conducting a Funeral

1. The funeral service should be characterized by orderliness, simplicity, and brevity. Herein are the secrets of successful and gratifying work in performing this difficult and delicate task. Simplicity without order will leave its unsatisfying impression on the minds of the bereaved and orderliness without simplicity may irk the bereaved and tire them by its length.

2. The purpose of the funeral service is to calm and soothe the bereaved. It is the duty of the minister to use such aids and so to conduct the services as to promote calmness in the breasts of the bereaved. Therefore, he should avoid the use of any language in the prayer, address, or sermon, the use of any hymn or poetry or even Scripture, which is calculated to harrow the feelings of the bereaved or to re-open their wounds. Experience goes to show that Scripture plays the most important part in bringing comfort to those in sorrow. Accordingly it should be given the

major place in the funeral service. More time may be spent in reading the Scriptures than in any other feature of the service. Next to the Scriptures in importance is prayer. This should be neither too short nor too long, and above all things it should not be florid.

3. If hymns are used, they should be chosen with extreme discretion, for their singing usually serves as an intimate reminder of the departed one and thus gives rise to renewed outbursts of grief. Old hymns are the best.

4. As to the address or sermon, it should be borne in mind that brevity is a real virtue. Ten minutes are sufficient for any sermon or address unless the departed is of unusual prominence. The address or sermon should never be eulogistic for two reasons: First, however kind the things said about the dead, they are never sufficiently glowing to the overwrought feelings of the bereaved. On the other hand, such kind remarks may seem overdrawn to those who are not bereaved and may prove a matter of embarrassment to the minister in his dealings with the latter. The writer believes that nothing but the gospel or some feature thereof ought to be the subject of a funeral address or sermon, and of these subjects the resurrection is the best. A list of suitable texts will be found in the follow-

ing pages. And volumes of Funeral Sermons and Memorial Addresses are now available. Every young minister should have one or more such volumes.

5. When a minister is invited to conduct a funeral, he should at once undertake to make himself thoroughly conversant with the circumstances and religious history of the departed and of the family. Of course, if the departed is a member of the minister's congregation, he will already have these facts in hand, but if the minister is called to conduct the funeral of a stranger, when possible, he should visit the house before the funeral, become acquainted with the members of the family or interested persons, and ascertain such facts as he considers needful. If this is not possible, he should go some minutes before the hour set and meet the members of the family or interested persons and obtain the needful information.

6. There is some difference of opinion as to which is better: conducting the funeral from the residence or from the church. Undoubtedly the church is the best place because there all may be seated in comfort. But a church funeral implies length and dignity, as well as publicity, and from all three of these most families shrink. Accordingly, most of the fu-

nerals are now conducted from residences. Perhaps this is well since it makes possible very brief exercises. But while brevity is desirable, the funeral should be so conducted as to leave the impression that all possible has been done to provide exercises worthy of the subject and occasion. In this connection, it may be noted that funeral customs vary widely in different sections of the country. For instance, the writer knows of one city where a funeral address or sermon is never heard and where nothing more than scripture reading, prayer, and singing of hymns ever occurs at any funeral service. On the other hand, the writer also knows of many communities where nothing short of an hour and a half funeral meets the demand of the people. Both these cases are extreme, but the former is the more desirable. Where the customs seem improper when judged by the best standards of usage, the minister, by discreet effort, should seek to procure proper and dignified observances. Consultation with the funeral director and an understanding with him will usually bring about the desired changes with the minimum of trouble. Sympathetic co-operation between minister and funeral director can accomplish much.

7. The deportment of the minister at the funeral is a matter of importance. If it is a church funeral, shall he enter the church leading the pallbearers and the casket or shall he occupy the pulpit and await the coming of the funeral party? If the church is a large one and has an organ and the organist is prepared to render a funeral march, it is better for the minister to occupy the pulpit and simply await the coming of the funeral party into the church. If, however, there is to be no funeral march, it is entirely proper for the minister to meet the funeral party at the door of the church and, leading the procession into the church, read or quote such scripture as may seem appropriate. When the services of the church funeral are concluded, it is proper for the minister to take his place in the advance of the pallbearers and thus quietly lead the funeral party from the church. Upon arriving at the tomb, the minister should take his place at the head of the funeral party and continue such exercises or read such scriptures as have been suggested or as may seem proper. The deportment of the minister at the residence funeral upon its conclusion should be the same as that of the church funeral just described. In some cities and on some occasions the minister will not be re-

quired to go to the cemetery, but generally speaking in the South it is expected of him, and, unless there is good reason for him to remain away, he should by all means go.

8. Another feature which should have the careful attention of the minister and the funeral director is that of warning friends and others not to approach the bereaved while the funeral exercises are in progress.   At the home or the church friends should not approach the bereaved upon conclusion of the exercises. If such approaches are made they will result in nothing but confusion and disorder and will hinder, rather than help the bereaved. At the cemetery, after the benediction is said, is the proper time for friends to go forward and speak words of comfort and condolence.   Then such attentions are both appropriate and highly desirable and will produce the best measure of help that can be offered on the occasion of the funeral.   Co-operation between the minister and the funeral director will procure this without offense to anyone.

9. In this connection it must be said that the minister's deportment in the sick room and at the death bed are exceedingly important. No rules can be laid down to govern the minister at such a time because each instance

will present features quite different from all others. Physicians are usually very impatient of the presence of ministers with patients seriously ill; especially so if the minister insists upon reading the Bible or offering prayer, which in the judgment of the physician will disturb the patient and produce harmful results. If the patient or family asks for prayer and scripture reading, then the minister may proceed. Otherwise it is better simply to be near at hand to offer what help may seem advisable as the occasion may seem to demand. The minister should be very discreet and ready for whatever is needed and proper in the circumstances. Appropriate scripture may be found in the "services" which follow, and circumstances should dictate the nature of the prayer.

10. The minister should always call at the home very soon after the funeral to offer consolation and counsel. If some small volume of sermons or essays calculated to comfort the reader is available, he should present a copy thereof to the family or bereaved individuals, asking them to read it for comfort and help. This is a very delicate service to render, but where it is rendered with tact and in the true spirit of the Master, it will give the minister a hold upon the bereaved that can be had no

other way. He should prepare himself for such service with care and should not neglect its performance in any way.

11. In the following pages will be found a number of "Funeral Services." These have been prepared more for the purpose of providing suggestive models than for use outright by the minister. However, when a minister finds himself crowded for time and wishes some convenient form to use, he will find these models in most instances quite acceptable and he may use them outright with the utmost propriety. If the Scripture selections seem lengthy, he may omit certain portions. If, on the other hand, there are certain other scriptural selections which seem more appropriate to him, he may use them as substitutes. These models have not been hastily nor arbitrarily prepared. And they include most of the scriptural selections which are suitable for funeral purposes. In fact they are merely the forms used by the writer in his twenty years' experience as a pastor. They have grown up with his experience and thus through the years have gradually assumed their proper form.

12. Very often the minister will find himself under the necessity of conducting the funeral service in connection with some order

such as the Masons, Odd Fellows, Confederate Veterans, and so forth. The author had thought to prepare a joint service for the several orders, but there are so many of them that such an effort would be impracticable. However, such joint services may be conducted without conflict and in due order by the simple device of having an understanding before the funeral just what part the minister is to perform and just what part the representatives of the order are to perform. Usually the Masons care to have only the exercises at the grave in their charge. In this case the minister's part is concluded at the residence or church. Every minister should acquaint himself fully with the wishes of the family and of the order, and having done so should reach an exact agreement with those in charge as to the parts which each is to be responsible for and when. It is better to follow the Masonic custom and give the entire ceremony at the grave to the order, reserving the ceremonies of the home or church for the minister. Where the minister happens to be a member of the order himself he may act the part of chaplain to the order and thus have part in all the exercises.

13. There seems to be an increasing demand for suitable poetry to use in funeral

services. Consequently a collection is found in this little volume. Space forbids that it should be a large collection, and the author well knows that the choice of poetry is largely a matter of taste. It is hoped, however, that the poems included will appeal to the ministry and will furnish them what they need in this line. There are now volumes of poetry collected to supply this very demand and each minister should provide himself with a copy of such collection.

Funeral Service for General Purposes

The minister may say:

"But as it is written, things which eye saw not, and ear heard not, and which entered not into the heart of man, whatsoever things God prepared for them that love him. But unto us God revealed them through the Spirit; for the Spirit searcheth all things, yea, the deep things of God" (1 Cor. 2: 9, 10).

"Blessed is the man whom thou chastenest, O Jehovah, and teachest out of thy law; that thou mayest give him rest from the days of adversity, until the pit be digged for the wicked. For Jehovah will not cast off his people, neither will he forsake his inheritance" (Psalm 94: 12-14).

"Behold happy is the man whom God correcteth: therefore despise not thou the chastening of the Almighty" (Job 5: 17).

"For thou, O Jehovah, art my refuge! Thou hast made the Most High thy habitation:

there shall no evil befall thee, neither shall any plague come nigh thy tent. For he will give his angels charge over thee, to keep thee in all thy ways. They shall bear thee up in their hands, lest thou dash thy foot against a stone. Thou shalt tread upon the lion and adder: the young lion and the serpent shalt thou trample under foot. Because he hath set his love upon me, therefore will I deliver him: I will set him on high, because he hath known my name. He shall call upon me, and I will answer him; I will be with him in trouble: I will deliver him and honor him" (Psalm 91: 9-15).

Hymn—(May be sung or read, or suitable poetry may be used instead.)

Then the minister may say:

Beloved, let us seek comfort in the assurances of God's Word.

If we would be assured of God's care for us, heed the following precious words:

"Jehovah is my shepherd; I shall not want. He maketh me to lie down in green pastures; He leadeth me beside still waters. He restoreth my soul: He guideth me in the paths of righteousness for his name's sake. Yea, though I walk through the valley of the shadow of death, I will fear no evil; for thou art with

me; thy rod and thy staff, they comfort me.
Thou preparest a table before me in the presence of mine enemies. Thou hast anointed my
head with oil; my cup runneth over. Surely
goodness and lovingkindness shall follow me
all the days of my life; and I shall dwell in the
house of Jehovah for ever" (Psalm 23).

If we would be assured of ultimate triumph
of God's people let us hear these other precious words:

"For I reckon that the sufferings of this
present time are not worthy to be compared
with the glory which shall be revealed to us-
ward. For the earnest expectation of the
creation waiteth for the revealing of the sons
of God. For the creation was subjected to
vanity, not of its own will, but by reason of
him who subjected it, in hope that the creation
itself also shall be delivered from the bondage
of corruption into the liberty of the glory of
the children of God. For we know that the
whole creation groaneth and travaileth in pain
together unto now. And not only so, but ourselves also, who have the first fruits of the
Spirit even we ourselves groan within ourselves waiting for our adoption, to wit, the redemption of our body. For in hope were we
saved: but hope that is seen is not hope: for
who hopeth for that which he seeth? But if we

hope for that which we see not, then do we with patience wait for it.

"And in like manner the Spirit also helpeth our infirmity: for we know not how to pray as we ought; but the Spirit himself maketh intercession for us with groanings which cannot be uttered; and he that searcheth the hearts knoweth what is the mind of the Spirit, because he maketh intercession for the saints according to the will of God. And we know that to them that love God all things work together for good, even to them that are called according to his purpose. For whom he foreknew, he also foreordained to be conformed to the image of his Son, that he might be the firstborn among many brethren: and whom he foreordained, them he also called: and whom he called, them he also justified: and whom he justified, them he also glorified.

"What then shall we say to these things? If God is for us, who is against us? He that spared not his own Son, but delivered him up for us all, how shall he not also with him freely give us all things? Who shall lay anything to the charge of God's elect? It is God that justifieth; who is he that condemneth? It is Christ Jesus that died, yea rather, that was raised from the dead, who is at the right hand of God, who also maketh intercession for us. Who shall separate us from the love of Christ? Shall tribulation, or anguish, or persecution, or famine, or nakedness, or peril, or sword? Even as it is written,

For thy sake we are killed all the day long;
We were accounted as sheep for the slaughter,

Nay, in all these things we are more than conquerors through him that loved us. For I am persuaded, that neither death, nor life, nor angels, nor principalities, nor things present, nor things to come, nor powers, nor height, nor depth, nor any other creature, shall be able to separate us from the love of God, which is in Christ Jesus our Lord" (Rom. 8: 18-39).

If we would be assured of the blessedness of tribulations, let us hear the following comforting words:

"And one of the elders answered, saying unto me, These that are arrayed in the white robes, who are they and whence came they? And I say unto him, My Lord, thou knowest. And he said to me, these are they that come out of the great tribulation, and they washed their robes, and made them white in the blood of the Lamb. Therefore are they before the throne of God; and they serve him day and night in his temple: and he that sitteth on the throne shall spread his tabernacle over them. They shall hunger no more, neither thirst any more; neither shall the sun strike upon them, nor any heat: for the Lamb that is in the midst of the throne shall be their shepherd, and shall guide them unto fountains of waters of life: and God shall wipe away every tear from their eyes" (Rev. 7: 13-17).

If we would be assured of an abiding home let our hearts be consoled by these words:

"Let not your heart be troubled: believe in God, believe also in me. In my Father's house are many mansions; if it were not so, I would have told you; for I go to prepare a place for you. And if I go and prepare a place for you, I come again, and will receive you unto myself; that where I am, there ye may be also" (John 14: 1-3).

If we would be assured of the coming again of our Lord and the resurrection, let our hearts be stayed on the following words:

"But we would not have you ignorant, brethren, concerning them that fall asleep; that ye sorrow not, even as the rest, who have no hope. For if we believe that Jesus died and rose again, even so them also that are fallen asleep in Jesus will God bring with him. For this we say unto you by the word of the Lord, that we that are alive, that are left unto the coming of the Lord, shall in no wise precede them that are fallen asleep. For the Lord, himself shall descend from heaven, with a shout, with the voice of the archangel, and with the trump of God: and the dead in Christ shall rise first; then we that are alive, that are left, shall together with them be caught up in the clouds, to meet the Lord in the air: and so shall we ever be with the Lord. Wherefore comfort one another with these words" (1 Thess. 4: 13-18).

Then the minister may say:

Having heard God speaking to us in his Word, let us now take our sorrow to him, being assured that he will hear us by the following blessed words:

"Draw nigh to God and he will draw nigh to you. Cleanse your hands, ye sinners, and purify your hearts, ye double minded. . . . Humble yourselves in the sight of the Lord, and he shall exalt you" (James 4: 8, 10).

Prayer.

Hymn—(May be sung or read, or suitable poetry may be used instead).

Address—(If deemed advisable).

Hymn—(May be sung or read, or suitable poetry may be used instead).

Then the minister may say:

The services here are now concluded, **and** we will repair to the cemetery where the interment will take place.

(Minister takes place in lead of pallbearers and walks from home or church in this order to the funeral carriage. Upon arrival at the cemetery the minister again takes his place in the lead of the pallbearers and walks in this order to the grave).

Then the minister may say (as he walks in the lead of the procession):

"And I heard a voice from heaven saying, Write, Blessed are the dead who die in the Lord from henceforth: yea, saith the Spirit, that they may rest from their labors; for their works follow with them" (Rev. 14: 13).

"Thou wilt guide me with thy counsel, and afterward receive me to glory. Whom have I in heaven but thee? And there is none upon earth that I desire besides thee. My flesh and my heart faileth; but God is the strength of my heart and my portion for ever" (Psalm 73: 24-26).

(When the casket has been placed on the supports ready for lowering into the grave, the minister takes his stand at the head of the grave).

Then the minister may say (as the casket is lowered):

"Now this I say, brethren, that flesh and blood cannot inherit the kingdom of God;

neither doth corruption inherit incorruption. Behold, I tell you a mystery: we all shall not sleep, but we shall all be changed, in a moment, in the twinkling of an eye, at the last trump: for the trumpet shall sound, and the dead shall be raised incorruptible, and we shall be changed. For this corruptible must put on incorruption, and this mortal must put on immortality. But when this corruptible shall have put on incorruption, and this mortal shall have put on immortality, then shall come to pass the saying that is written, Death is swallowed up in victory. O death, where is thy victory? O death, where is thy sting? The sting of death is sin; and the power of sin is the law: but thanks be to God, who giveth us the victory through our Lord Jesus Christ. Wherefore, my beloved brethren, be ye stedfast, unmovable, always abounding in the work of the Lord, forasmuch as ye know that your labor is not vain in the Lord" (1 Cor. 15: 50-58).

Then the minister may use the following committal service:

My Friends: Whereas, death hath once more invaded our ranks and removed from the walks of life our beloved Brother (or Sister)——————, his (or her) soul having departed to dwell in "The undiscovered country from whose bourn no traveler returns," it has become our sad duty to commit his (or her) body to the grave: Earth to earth, ashes to ashes, dust to dust, and our inspiring privilege to commend his (or her) soul to our Maker, Father, and Redeemer, in the confident hope of the coming again of our Lord and Saviour Jesus Christ, the resurrection of the body from the grave, and the joyous life reserved for the children of light in the realms of glory.

(Then the grave may be filled or canopied and decorated with flowers. After which the people may be dismissed by prayer or benediction).

Dismissing the people the minister may say:

"The peace of God, which passeth all understanding, shall guard your hearts and your thoughts in Christ Jesus. . . . Now unto our God and Father be the glory for ever and ever. Amen" (Phil. 4: 7, 20).

Funeral Service for a Child

OPENING:

The minister may say:

"For our light affliction, which is for the moment, worketh for us more and more exceedingly an eternal weight of glory; while we look not at the things which are seen, but at the things which are not seen: for the things which are seen are temporal; but the things which are not seen are eternal" (2 Cor. 4: 17, 18).

Hymn—(May be sung or read, or suitable poetry may be used instead).

Then the minister may say:

We seek comfort, let us find it in the Scriptures. If we would be comforted in our knowledge of our Lord's love for children, let us heed the following:

"And they were bringing unto him little children, that he should touch them: and the disciples rebuked them. But when Jesus saw it, he was moved with indignation, and said

unto them, suffer the little children to come
unto me; forbid them not: for to such belongeth the kingdom of God. Verily I say
unto you, whosoever shall not receive the kingdom of God as a little child, he shall in no wise
enter therein. And he took them in his arms,
and blessed them, laying his hands upon
them" (Mark 10: 13-16).

"In that hour came the disciples unto Jesus,
saying, Who then is greatest in the kingdom of
heaven? And he called to him a little child,
and set him in the midst of them, and said,
Verily I say unto you, Except ye turn and become as little children, ye shall in no wise
enter into the kingdom of heaven. Whosoever therefore shall humble himself as this
little child, the same is the greatest in the kingdom of heaven. And whoso shall receive one
such little child in my name receiveth me:
but whoso shall cause one of these little ones
that believe on me to stumble, it is profitable
for him that a great millstone should be
hanged about his neck, and that he should be
sunk in the depth of the sea" (Matt. 18:
1-6).

"See that ye despise not one of these little
ones: for I say unto you, that in heaven their
angels do always behold the face of my Father who is in heaven. How think ye? if any

man have a hundred sheep and one of them be gone astray, doth he not leave the ninety and nine, and go unto the mountains, and seek that which goeth astray. And if so be that he find it, verily I say unto you, he rejoiceth over it more than over the ninety and nine which have not gone astray. Even so it is not the will of your Father who is in heaven, that one of these little ones should perish" (Matt. 18: 10-14).

If we would be comforted in a Bible example of grief for a child properly borne, let us heed:

"And it came to pass on the seventh day, that the child died. And the servants of David feared to tell him that the child was dead; for they said, Behold, while the child was yet alive, we spake unto him, and he hearkened not unto our voice: how will he then vex himself, if we tell him that the child is dead! But when David saw that his servants were whispering together, David perceived that the child was dead; and David said unto his servants, Is the child dead? And they said, He is dead. Then David arose from the earth, and washed and anointed himself, and changed his apparel; and he came into the house of Jehovah, and worshiped: then he came to his own house; and when he required, they set bread before him, and he did eat. Then said his servants unto him, What thing is this that thou hast done? Thou didst fast and weep for the child, when it was alive; but when the child was dead, thou didst rise and eat bread. And he said, While the child was yet alive, I fasted and wept: for I said, Who knoweth whether Jehovah will not be gracious to me, that the child may live? But now he is dead, wherefore should I fast? Can I bring him back again? I shall go to him, but he will not return to me" (2 Samuel 12: 18-23).

If we would be comforted in what God has in store for us, let us heed:

"Let not your heart be troubled: believe in God, believe also in me. In my Father's house are many mansions; if it were not so, I would have told you; for I go to prepare a place for you. And if I go and prepare a place for you, I come again, and will receive you unto myself; that where I am, there ye may be also. And whither I go, ye know the way" (John 14: 1-4).

"And he showed me a river of water of life, bright as crystal, proceeding out of the throne of God and of the Lamb, in the midst of the street thereof. And on this side of the river and on that was the tree of life, bearing twelve manner of fruits, yielding its fruit

every month: and the leaves of the tree were
for the healing of the nations.   And there shall
be no curse any more: and the throne of God
and of the Lamb shall be therein: and his
servants shall serve him; and they shall see
his face; and his name shall be on their fore-
heads.   And there shall be night no more;
and they need no light of lamp, neither light
of sun; for the Lord God shall give them light:
and they shall reign for ever and ever" (Rev.
22: 1-5).

Then the minister may say:

Having heard God speaking to us in his
Word, let us now take our sorrow to him, being assured that he will hear us by the following blessed words:

"Draw nigh to God and he will draw nigh
to you.   Cleanse your hands, ye sinners; and
purify your hearts, ye doubleminded. . . .
Humble yourselves in the sight of the Lord,
and he shall exalt you" (James 4: 8, 10).

Prayer.

Hymn—(May be sung or read, or suitable
poetry may be used instead).

Address—(If deemed advisable).

Hymn—(May be sung or read, or suitable
poetry may be used instead).

Then the minister may say:

The services here are now concluded, and we will repair to the cemetery where the interment will take place.

(Minister takes place in lead of pallbearers and walks from home or church in this order to the funeral carriage. Upon arrival at the cemetery the minister again takes his place in the lead of the pallbearers and walks in this order to the grave).

Then the minister may say (as he walks in the lead of the procession):

"And I heard a voice from heaven saying, Write, Blessed are the dead who die in the Lord from henceforth: yea, saith the Spirit, that they may rest from their labors; for their works follow with them" (Rev. 14: 13).

"Thou wilt guide me with thy counsel, and afterward receive me to glory. Whom have I in heaven but thee? And there is none upon earth that I desire besides thee. My flesh and my heart faileth; but God is the strength of my heart and my portion for ever" (Psalm 73: 24-26).

(When the casket has been placed on the supports ready for lowering into the grave, the minister takes his stand at the head of the grave).

Then the minister may say (as the casket is lowered):

"Now this I say, brethren, that flesh and blood cannot inherit the kingdom of God;

neither doth corruption inherit incorruption. Behold, I tell you a mystery: we all shall not sleep, but we shall all be changed, in a moment, in the twinkling of an eye, at the last trump: for the trumpet shall sound and the dead shall be raised incorruptible, and we shall be changed. For this corruptible must put on incorruption, and this mortal must put on immortality. But when this corruptible shall have put on incorruption, and this mortal shall have put on immortality, then shall come to pass the saying that is written, Death is swallowed up in victory. O death, where is thy victory? O death, where is thy sting? The sting of death is sin; and the power of sin is the law: but thanks be to God, who giveth us the victory through our Lord Jesus Christ. Wherefore, my beloved brethren, be ye stedfast, unmovable, always abounding in the work of the Lord, forasmuch as ye know that your labor is not vain in the Lord" (1 Cor. 15: 50-58).

Then the minister may use the following committal service:

My Friends: Whereas, death hath once more invaded our ranks and removed from the walks of life our beloved Brother (or Sister)——————, his (or her) soul having departed to dwell in "The undiscovered country from whose bourn no traveler returns," it has become our sad duty to commit his (or her) body to the grave: Earth to earth, ashes to ashes, dust to dust, and our inspiring privilege to commend his (or her) soul to our Maker, Father, and Redeemer, in the confident hope of the coming again of our Lord and Saviour Jesus Christ, the resurrection of the body from the grave, and the joyous life reserved for the children of light in the realms of glory.

(Then the grave may be filled or canopied and decorated with flowers. After which the people may be dismissed by prayer or benediction).

Dismissing the people the minister may say:

"The peace of God, which passeth all understanding, shall guard your hearts and your thoughts in Christ Jesus. . . . Now unto our God and Father be the glory for ever and ever. Amen" (Phil. 4: 7, 20).

Funeral Service for a Young Man

OPENING:

The minister may say:

"For it is as when a man going into another country, called his own servants, and delivered unto them his goods. And unto one he gave five talents, to another two, to another one; to each according to his several ability; and he went on his journey. Straightway he that received the five talents went and traded with them, and made other five talents. In like manner he also that received the two gained other two. But he that received the one went away and digged in the earth, and hid his lord's money. Now after a long time the lord of those servants cometh, and maketh a reckoning with them. And he that received the five talents came and brought other five talents, saying, Lord, thou deliveredst unto me five talents: lo, I have gained other five talents. His lord said unto him, Well done, good and faithful servant: thou hast been faithful over a few things, I will set thee over many things;

enter thou into the joy of thy lord. And he also that received the two talents came and said, Lord, thou deliveredst unto me two talents: lo, I have gained other two talents. His lord said unto him, Well done, good and faithful servant, thou hast been faithful over a few things, I will set thee over many things; enter thou into the joy of thy lord" (Matt. 25: 14-23).

Hymn—(May be sung or read, or suitable poetry may be used instead).

Then the minister may say:

Beloved, let us find comfort in the Word of God.

If we would be comforted in the hope for a young man as evidenced by the voice and acts of Jesus, let us heed the following words:

"Thomas therefore, who is called Didymus, said unto his fellow disciples, Let us also go, that we may die with him. So when Jesus came, he found that he had been in the tomb four days already. Now Bethany was nigh unto Jerusalem, about fifteen furlongs off; and many of the Jews had come to Martha and Mary, to console them concerning their brother. Martha, therefore, when she heard that Jesus was coming, went and met him: but Mary still sat in the house. Martha therefore said unto Jesus, Lord, if thou hadst been here, my brother had not died. And even now I know that, whatsoever thou shalt ask of God, God will give thee. Jesus saith unto her, Thy brother shall rise again. Martha saith unto him, I know that he shall rise again in the resurrection at the last day. Jesus said unto her, I am the resurrection, and the life: he that believeth on me, though he die, yet shall he live; and whosoever liveth and believeth on me shall never die. Believest thou this? She saith unto him, Yea, Lord; I have believed that thou art the Christ, the Son of God, even he that cometh into the world. And when she had said this, she went away, and called Mary her sister secretly, saying, The Teacher is here, and calleth thee. And she, when she heard it, arose quickly, and went unto him. (Now Jesus was not yet come into the village, but was still in the place where Martha met him). The Jews then who were with her in the house, and were consoling her, when they saw Mary, that she rose up quickly and went out, followed her, supposing that she was going unto the tomb to weep there. Mary, therefore, when she came where Jesus was, and saw him, fell down at his feet, saying unto him, Lord, if thou hadst been here, my brother had not died. When Jesus, therefore, saw her weeping, and the Jews also weeping, who came with her, he groaned in the spirit and was troubled, and said, Where have ye laid him? They say unto him, Lord, come and see. Jesus wept. The Jews, therefore, said, Behold how he loved him! But some of them said, Could not this man, who opened the eyes of him that was blind, have caused that this man also should not die? Jesus therefore again groaning in himself cometh to the tomb. Now it was a cave, and a stone lay against it. Jesus saith, Take ye away the stone. Martha, the sister of him that was dead, saith unto him, Lord, by this time the body decayeth; for he hath been dead four days. Jesus saith unto her, Said I not unto thee, that, if thou believedst, thou shouldest see the glory of God? So they took away the stone. And Jesus lifted up his eyes, and said, Father, I thank thee that thou heardest me. And I knew that thou hearest me always: but because of the multitude that standeth around I said it, that they may believe that thou didst send me. And when he had thus spoken, he cried with a loud voice, Lazarus, come forth. He that was dead came forth, bound hand and foot with graveclothes; and his face was bound about with a napkin. Jesus saith unto them, Loose him and let him go.

"Many therefore of the Jews, who came to Mary and beheld that which he did, believed on him. But some of them went away to the Pharisees, and told them the things which Jesus had done" (John 11: 16-46).

Let us be comforted in the following Scripture for if Jesus raised the widow's son so will he some day raise all other sons who have died in him:

"And it came to pass soon afterwards, that he went to a city called Nain; and his disciples went with him, and a great multitude. Now when he drew near to the gate of the city, behold, there was carried out one that was dead, the only son of his mother, and she was a widow: and much people of the city was with her. And when the Lord saw her, he had compassion on her, and said unto her, Weep not. And he came nigh and touched the bier: and the bearers stood still. And he said, Young man, I say unto thee, Arise. And he that was dead sat up, and began to speak. And he gave him to his mother" (Luke 7: 11-15).

Then the minister may say.

Having heard God speaking to us in his Word, let us now take our sorrow to him, being assured that he will hear us by the following blessed words:

"Draw nigh to God, and he will draw nigh to you.   Cleanse your hands, ye sinners; and purify your hearts, ye doubleminded. . . . Humble yourselves in the sight of the Lord, and he shall exalt you" (James 4: 8, 10).

Prayer.

Hymn—(May be sung or read, or suitable poetry may be used instead).

Address—(If deemed advisable).

Hymn—(May be sung or read, or suitable poetry may be used instead).

Then the minister may say:

The services here are now concluded, and we will repair to the cemetery where the interment will take place.

(Minister takes place in lead of pallbearers and walks from home or church in this order to the funeral carriage. Upon arrival at the cemetery the minister again takes his place in the lead of the pallbearers and walks in this order to the grave).

Then the minister may say (as he walks in the lead of the procession):

"And I heard a voice from heaven saying, Write, Blessed are the dead who die in the Lord from henceforth: yea, saith the Spirit, that they may rest from their labors; for their works follow with them" (Rev. 14: 13).

"Thou wilt guide me with thy counsel, and afterward receive me to glory. Whom have I in heaven but thee? And there is none upon earth that I desire besides thee. My flesh and my heart faileth; but God is the strength of my heart and my portion for ever" (Psalm 73: 24-26).

(When the casket has been placed on the supports ready for lowering into the grave, the minister takes his stand at the head of the grave.)

Then the minister may say (as the casket is lowered):

"Now this I say, brethren, that flesh and blood cannot inherit the kingdom of God; neither doth corruption inherit incorruption. Behold, I tell you a mystery: we all shall not sleep, but we shall all be changed, in a moment, in the twinkling of an eye, at the last trump: for the trumpet shall sound, and the dead shall be raised incorruptible, and we shall be changed. For this corruptible must put on incorruption, and this mortal must put on immortality. But when this corruptible shall have put on incorruption, and this mortal shall have put on immortality, then shall come to pass the saying that is written, Death is swallowed up in victory. O death, where is thy victory? O death, where is thy sting? The sting of death is sin; and the power of sin is the law: but thanks be to God, who giveth us the victory through our Lord Jesus Christ. Wherefore, my beloved brethren, be ye stedfast, unmovable, always abounding in the work of the Lord, forasmuch as ye know that your labor is not vain in the Lord" (1 Cor. 15: 50-58).

Then the minister may use the following committal service:

My Friends: Whereas, death hath once more invaded our ranks and removed from the walks of life our beloved Brother ————, his soul having departed to dwell in "The undiscovered country from whose bourn no traveler returns," it has become our sad duty to commit his body to the grave: Earth to earth, ashes to ashes, dust to dust, and our inspiring privilege to commend his soul to our Maker, Father, and Redeemer, in the confident hope of the coming again of our Lord and Saviour Jesus Christ, the resurrection of the body from the grave, and the joyous life reserved for the children of light in the realms of glory.

(Then the grave may be filled or canopied and decorated with flowers. After which the people may be dismissed by prayer or benediction).

Dismissing the people the minister may say:

"The peace of God, which passeth all understanding, shall guard your hearts and your thoughts in Christ Jesus. . . . Now unto our God and Father be the glory for ever and ever. Amen" (Phil. 4: 7, 20).

Funeral Service for a Young Woman

OPENING:

The minister may say:

"There hath no temptation taken you but such as man can bear: but God is faithful, who will not suffer you to be tempted above that ye are able; but will with the temptation make also the way of escape, that ye may be able to endure it" (1 Cor. 10: 13).

"Blessed be the God and Father of our Lord Jesus Christ, the Father of mercies and God of all comfort; who comforteth us in all our affliction, that we may be able to comfort them that are in any affliction, through the comfort wherewith we ourselves are comforted of God. For as the sufferings of Christ abound unto us, even so our comfort also aboundeth through Christ. But whether we are afflicted, it is for your comfort and salvation; or whether we are comforted, it is for your comfort, which worketh in the patient enduring of the same sufferings which we also suffer: and our hope for you is stedfast; knowing that, as ye are partakers of the sufferings, so also are ye of the comfort" (2 Cor. 1: 3-7).

"For the Lord will not cast off for ever. For though he cause grief, yet will he have compassion according to the multitude of his lovingkindnesses. For he doth not afflict willingly, nor grieve the children of men" (Lam. 3: 31-33).

"Like as a father pitieth his children, so Jehovah pitieth them that fear him. For he knoweth our frame; he remembereth that we are dust" (Psalm 103: 13, 14).

Hymn—(May be sung or read, or suitable poetry may be used instead).

Then the minister may say:

Beloved, let us seek comfort in the assurances of God's Word.

If we would be assured that God hath prepared comfort for us, let us hear reverently the following blessed words:

"The Spirit of the Lord Jehovah is upon me; because Jehovah hath anointed me to preach good tidings unto the meek; he hath sent me to bind up the broken hearted, to proclaim liberty to the captives, and the opening of the prison to them that are bound; to proclaim the year of Jehovah's favor, and the day of vengeance of our God; to comfort all

that mourn; to appoint unto them that mourn
in Zion, to give unto them a garland for ashes,
the oil of joy for mourning, the garment of
praise for the spirit of heaviness; that they
may be called trees of righteousness, the plant-
ing of Jehovah, that he may be glorified"
(Isa. 61: 1-3).

"And I will pray the Father, and he shall
give you another Comforter, that he may be
with you for ever, even the Spirit of truth:
whom the world cannot receive; for it beholdeth him not, neither knoweth him: ye
know him; for he abideth with you, and shall
be in you. I will not leave you desolate: I
come unto you. Yet a little while, and the
world beholdeth me no more; but ye behold
me: because I live, ye shall live also" (John
14: 16-19).

If we would be assured of God's special
care for such as the one we mourn today, let
us hear the following beautiful story and other
reassuring promises:

"And there cometh one of the rulers of the
synagogue, Jairus by name; and seeing him,
he falleth at his feet, and beseecheth him
much, saying, My little daughter is at the
point of death: I pray thee, that thou come
and lay thy hands on her, that she may be
made whole, and live. And he went with him;

and a great multitude followed him, and they
thronged him. . . . While he yet spake,
they come from the ruler of the synagogue's
house, saying, Thy daughter is dead: why
troublest thou the Teacher any further?   But
Jesus, not heeding the word spoken, saith unto
the ruler of the synagogue, Fear not, only believe.   And he suffered no man to follow with
him, save Peter, and James, and John the
brother of James.   And they come to the
house of the ruler of the synagogue; and he
beholdeth a tumult, and many weeping and
wailing greatly.   And when he was entered in,
he saith unto them, Why make ye a tumult and
weep? the child is not dead, but sleepeth.
And they laughed him to scorn.   But he, having put them all forth, taketh the father of
the child and her mother and them that were
with him, and goeth in where the child was.
And taking the child by the hand, he saith
unto her, Talitha cumi; which is, being interpreted, Damsel, I say unto thee, Arise.   And
straightway the damsel rose up, and walked;
for she was twelve years old.   And they were
amazed straightway with a great amazement"
(Mark 5: 22-24; 35-42).

If we would be assured that we shall live
again—that there is no death for the righteous,

let us be comforted in the following Scriptures:

"Martha saith unto him, I know that he shall rise again in the resurrection at the last day. Jesus said unto her, I am the resurrection and the life: he that believeth on me, though he die, yet shall he live; and whosoever liveth and believeth on me shall never die. Believest thou this?" (John 11: 24-26).

"Verily, verily, I say unto you, the hour cometh and now is, when the dead shall hear the voice of the Son of God; and they that hear shall live. For as the Father hath life in himself, even so gave he to the Son also to have life in himself: and he gave him authority to execute judgment, because he is a son of man. Marvel not at this: for the hour cometh, in which all that are in the tombs shall hear his voice, and shall come forth; they that have done good, unto the resurrection of life; and they that have done evil, unto the resurrection of judgment" (John 5: 25-29).

"For our citizenship is in heaven; whence also we wait for a Saviour, the Lord Jesus Christ: who shall fashion anew the body of our humiliation, that it may be conformed to the body of his glory, according to the working whereby he is able even to subject all things unto himself" (Phil. 3: 20, 21).

Then the minister may say:

Having heard God speaking to us in his
Word, let us now take our sorrow to him being
assured that he will hear us by the following
blessed words:

"Draw nigh to God, and he will draw nigh
to you. Cleanse your hands, ye sinners; and
purify your hearts, ye doubleminded. . . .
Humble yourselves in the sight of the Lord,
and he shall exalt you" (James 4: 8, 10).

Prayer.

Hymn—(May be sung or read, or suitable
poetry may be used instead).

Address—(If deemed advisable).

Hymn—(May be sung or read, or suitable
poetry may be used instead).

Then the minister may say:

The services here are now concluded, and
we will repair to the cemetery where the interment will take place.

(Minister takes place in the lead of the pallbearers and walks from home or church in this
order to the funeral carriage. Upon arrival at the
cemetery the minister again takes his place in the
lead of the pallbearers and walks in this order to
the grave).

Then the minister may say (as he walks in the lead of the procession):

"And I heard a voice from heaven saying, Write, Blessed are the dead who die in the Lord from henceforth: yea, saith the Spirit, that they may rest from their labors; for their works follow with them" (Rev. 14: 13).

"Thou wilt guide me with thy counsel, and afterward receive me to glory. Whom have I in heaven but thee? And there is none upon earth that I desire besides thee. My flesh and my heart faileth; but God is the strength of my heart and my portion for ever" (Psalm 73: 24-26).

(When the casket has been placed on the supports ready for lowering into the grave, the minister takes his stand at the head of the grave).

Then the minister may say (as the casket is lowered):

"Now this I say, brethren, that flesh and blood cannot inherit the kingdom of God; neither doth corruption inherit incorruption. Behold, I tell you a mystery: we all shall not sleep, but we shall all be changed, in a moment, in the twinkling of an eye, at the last trump: for the trumpet shall sound, and the dead shall be raised incorruptible, and we shall be changed. For this corruptible must put on incorruption, and this mortal must put

on immortality. But when this corruptible
shall have put on incorruption, and this mortal shall have put on immortality, then shall
come to pass the saying that is written, Death
is swallowed up in victory. O death, where
is thy victory? O death, where is thy sting?
The sting of death is sin; and the power of
sin is the law: but thanks be to God, who giveth
us the victory through our Lord Jesus Christ.
Wherefore, my beloved brethren, be ye stedfast, unmovable, always abounding in the
work of the Lord, forasmuch as ye know that
your labor is not vain in the Lord" (1 Cor.
15: 50-58).

**Then the minister may use the following com-
mittal service:**

My Friends: Whereas, death hath once
more invaded our ranks and removed from
the walks of life our beloved Sister ———,
her soul having departed to dwell in "The
undiscovered country from whose bourn no
traveler returns," it has become our sad duty
to commit her body to the grave: Earth to
earth. ashes to ashes, dust to dust, and our inspiring privilege to commend her soul to our
Maker, Father, and Redeemer, in the confident
hope of the coming again of our Lord and

Saviour Jesus Christ, the resurrection of the body from the grave, and the joyous life reserved for the children of light in the realms of glory.

(Then the grave may be filled or canopied and decorated with flowers. After which the people may be dismissed by prayer or benediction).

Dismissing the people the minister may say:

"The peace of God, which passeth all understanding, shall guard your hearts and your thoughts in Christ Jesus. . . . Now unto our God and Father be the glory for ever and ever. Amen" (Phil. 4: 7, 20).

Funeral Service for Man or Woman in Middle Life

OPENING:

The minister may say:

"I waited patiently for Jehovah; and he inclined unto me, and heard my cry. He brought me up also out of a horrible pit, out of the miry clay; and he set my feet upon a rock, and established my goings. And he hath put a new song in my mouth, even praise unto our God: many shall see it, and fear, and shall trust in Jehovah" (Psalm 40: 1-3).

"Blessed be the God and Father of our Lord Jesus Christ, the Father of mercies and God of all comfort; who comforteth us in all our affliction, that we may be able to comfort them that are in any affliction, through the comfort wherewith we ourselves are comforted of God" (2 Cor. 1: 3, 4).

"When thou passest through the waters, I will be with thee; and through the rivers, they shall not overflow thee: when thou walkest through the fire, thou shalt not be burned, neither shall the flame kindle upon thee" (Isa. 43: 2).

"Behold what manner of love the Father hath bestowed upon us, that we should be called children of God; and such we are. For this cause the world knoweth us not, because it knew him not. Beloved, now are we children of God, and it is not yet made manifest what we shall be. We know that, if he shall be manifested, we shall be like him; for we shall see him even as he is" (1 John 3: 1, 2).

Hymn—(May be sung or read, or suitable poetry may be used instead).

Then the minister may say:

Beloved, let us seek comfort in the Word of God.

There is comfort in knowing that God overrules all for our good.

"Behold, happy is the man whom God correcteth: therefore despise not thou the chastening of the Almighty. For he maketh sore, and bindeth up; he woundeth, and his hands make whole. He will deliver thee in six troubles; yea, in seven there shall no evil touch thee. In famine he will redeem thee from death; and in war from the power of the sword. Thou shalt be hid from the scourge of the tongue; neither shalt thou be afraid of destruction when it cometh. At destruction and dearth thou shalt laugh; neither shalt thou be afraid of the beasts of the earth. For thou shalt be in league with the stones of the field; and the beasts of the field shall be at peace with thee. And thou shalt know that thy tent is in peace; and thou shalt visit thy fold, and shalt miss nothing. Thou shalt know also that thy seed shall be great, and thine offspring as the grass of the earth. Thou shalt come to thy grave in a full age, like as a shock of grain cometh in in its season. Lo this, we have searched it, so it is; hear it, and know thou it for thy good" (Job 5: 17-27).

Let us be comforted in that while life is frail there is security in God:

"Thou turnest man to destruction, and sayest, return, ye children of men. For a thousand years in thy sight are but as yesterday when it is past, and as a watch in the night. Thou carriest them away as with a flood; they are as a sleep: in the morning they are like grass which groweth up. In the morning it flourisheth, and groweth up; in the evening it is cut down, and withereth . . . . The days of our years are threescore years and ten, or even by reason of strength fourscore years: yet is their pride but labor and sorrow; for it is soon gone, and we fly away" (Psalm 90: 3-6, 10).

"For as in Adam all die, so also in Christ shall all be made alive. But each in his own order: Christ the first fruits; then they that are Christ's, at his coming. Then cometh the end, when he shall deliver up the kingdom to God, even the Father; when he shall have abolished all rule and all authority and power. For he must reign, till he hath put all his enemies under his feet. The last enemy that shall be abolished is death" (1 Cor. 15: 22-26).

Let us take comfort in the assurances the Scriptures give us concerning holy and faithful living:

"Finally, be strong in the Lord, and in the strength of his might. Put on the whole armor of God, that ye may be able to stand against the wiles of the devil. For our wrestling is not against flesh and blood, but against the principalities, against the powers, against the world-rulers of this darkness, against the spiritual hosts of wickedness in the heavenly places. Wherefore take up the whole armor of God, that ye may be able to withstand in the evil day, and, having done all, to stand. Stand therefore, having girded your loins with truth, and having put on the breastplate of righteousness, and having shod your feet with the preparation of the gospel of peace; withal taking up the shield of faith, wherewith ye shall be able to quench all the fiery darts of the evil one. And take the helmet of salvation, and the sword of the Spirit, which is the word of God: with all prayer and supplication praying at all seasons in the Spirit, and watching thereunto in all perseverance and supplication for all the saints" (Eph. 6: 10-18).

"Let your loins be girded about, and your lamps burning; and be ye yourselves like unto men looking for their lord, when he shall return from the marriage feast; that, when he cometh and knocketh, they may straightway open unto him. Blessed are those servants, whom the lord when he cometh shall find watching: verily I say unto you, that he shall gird himself, and make them sit down to meat, and shall come and serve them. And if he shall come in the second watch, and if in the third, and find them so, blessed are those servants. But know this, that if the master of the house had known in what hour the thief was coming, he would have watched, and not have left his house to be broken through. Be ye also ready: for in an hour that ye think not the Son of man cometh.

"And Peter said, Lord, speakest thou this parable unto us, or even unto all? And the Lord said, Who then is the faithful and wise steward, whom his lord shall set over his household, to give them their portion of food in due season? Blessed is that servant, whom his lord when he cometh shall find so doing. Of a truth I say unto you, that he will set him over all that he hath" (Luke 12: 35-44).

"Hear, my sons, the instruction of a father, and attend to know understanding: for I give you good doctrine; forsake ye not my law. For I was a son unto my father, tender and only beloved in the sight of my mother. And he taught me, and said unto me: Let thy heart retain my words; keep my commandments, and live; get wisdom, get understanding; forget not, neither decline from the words of my mouth; forsake her not, and she will preserve thee; love her, and she will keep thee. Wisdom is the principal thing; therefore get wisdom; yea, with all thy getting get understanding. Exalt her, and she will promote thee; she will bring thee to honor, when thou dost embrace her. She will give to thy head a chaplet of grace; a crown of beauty will she deliver to thee. Hear, O my Son, and receive my sayings; and the years of thy life shall be many. I have taught thee in the way of wisdom; I have led thee in paths of uprightness. When thou goest, thy steps shall not be straightened; and if thou runnest, thou shalt not stumble. Take fast hold of instruction; let her not go: keep her; for she is thy life. . . . My son, attend to my words; incline thine ear unto my sayings. Let them not depart from thine eyes; keep them in the midst of thy heart. For they are life unto those that find them, and health to all their flesh. Keep thy heart with all diligence; for out of it are the issues of life. Put away from thee a wayward mouth, and perverse lips put far from thee. Let thine eyes look right on, and let thine eyelids look straight before thee. Make level the path of thy feet, and let all thy ways be established. Turn not to the right hand nor to the left: remove thy foot from evil" (Prov. 4: 1-13; 20-27).

"But concerning the times and the seasons, brethren, ye have no need that aught be written unto you. For yourselves know perfectly that the day of the Lord so cometh as a thief in the night. When they are saying Peace and safety, then sudden destruction cometh upon them, as travail upon a woman with child; and they shall in no wise escape. But ye, brethren, are not in darkness, that that day should overtake you as a thief: for ye are all sons of light, and sons of the day: we are not of the night, nor of darkness; so then let us not sleep, as do the rest, but let us watch and be sober. For they that sleep, sleep in the night: and they that are drunken are drunken in the night. But let us, since we are of the day, be sober, putting on the breastplate of faith and love; and for a helmet, the hope of salvation. For God appointed us not unto wrath, but unto the obtaining of salvation through our Lord Jesus Christ, who died for us, that whether we wake or sleep, we should live together with him. Wherefore exhort one another, and build each other up, even as also ye do" (1 Thess. 5: 1-11).

Then the minister may say:

Having heard God speaking to us in his Word, let us now take our sorrow to him being assured that he will hear us by the following blessed words:

"Draw nigh to God, and he will draw nigh to you. Cleanse your hands, ye sinners; and purify your hearts, ye doubleminded. . . . Humble yourselves in the sight of the Lord, and he shall exalt you" (James 4: 8, 10).

Prayer.

Hymn—(May be sung or read, or suitable poetry may be used instead).

Address—(If deemed advisable).

Hymn—(May be sung or read, or suitable poetry may be used instead).

Then the minister may say:

The services here are now concluded, and
we will repair to the cemetery where the interment will take place.

(Minister takes place in the lead of pallbearers
and walks from home or church in this order to
the funeral carriage. Upon arrival at the cemetery
the minister again takes his place in the lead of
the pallbearers and walks in this order to the
grave).

**Then the minister may say (as he walks in the
lead of the procession):**

"And I heard a voice from heaven saying,
Write, Blessed are the dead who die in the
Lord from henceforth: yea, saith the Spirit,
that they may rest from their labors; for their
works follow with them." (Rev. 14: 13.)

"Thou wilt guide me with thy counsel, and
afterward receive me to glory. Whom have I
in heaven but thee? And there is none upon
earth that I desire besides thee. My flesh and
my heart faileth; but God is the strength of
my heart and my portion for ever" (Psalm
73: 24-26).

(When the casket has been placed on the supports ready for lowering into the grave, the minister takes his stand at the head of the grave).

Then the minister may say (as the casket is lowered):

"Now this I say, brethren, that flesh and blood cannot inherit the kingdom of God; neither doth corruption inherit incorruption. Behold, I tell you a mystery: we all shall not sleep, but we shall all be changed, in a moment, in the twinkling of an eye, at the last trump: for the trumpet shall sound, and the dead shall be raised incorruptible, and we shall be changed. For this corruptible must put on incorruption, and this mortal must put on immortality. But when this corruptible shall have put on incorruption, and this mortal shall have put on immortality, then shall come to pass the saying that is written, Death is swallowed up in victory. O death, where is thy victory? O death, where is thy sting? The sting of death is sin; and the power of sin is the law: but thanks be to God, who giveth us the victory through our Lord Jesus Christ. Wherefore, my beloved brethren, be ye stedfast, unmovable, always abounding in the work of the Lord, forasmuch as ye know that your labor is not vain in the Lord" (1 Cor. 15: 50-58).

Then the minister may use the following committal service:

My Friends: Whereas, death hath once more invaded our ranks and removed from the walks of life our beloved Brother (or Sister)—————, his (or her) soul having departed to dwell in "The undiscovered country from whose bourn no traveler returns," it has become our sad duty to commit his (or her) body to the grave: Earth to earth, ashes to ashes, dust to dust, and our inspiring privilege to commend his (or her) soul to our Maker, Father, and Redeemer, in the confident hope of the coming again of our Lord and Saviour Jesus Christ, the resurrection of the body from the grave, and the joyous life reserved for the children of light in the realms of glory.

(Then the grave may be filled or canopied and decorated with flowers. After which the people may be dismissed by prayer or benediction).

Dismissing the people the minister may say:

"The peace of God, which passeth all understanding, shall guard your hearts and your thoughts in Christ Jesus. . . . Now unto our God and Father be the glory for ever and ever. Amen" (Phil. 4: 7, 20).

Funeral Service for an Aged Man

OPENING:

The minister may say:

"For we know that if the earthly house of our tabernacle be dissolved, we have a building from God, a house not made with hands, eternal, in the heavens. For verily in this we groan, longing to be clothed upon with our habitation which is from heaven: if so be that being clothed we shall not be found naked. For indeed we that are in this tabernacle do groan, being burdened; not for that we would be unclothed, but that we would be clothed upon, that what is mortal may be swallowed up of life. Now he that wrought us for this very thing is God, who gave unto us the earnest of the Spirit. Being, therefore, always of good courage, and knowing that, whilst we are at home in the body, we are absent from the Lord (for we walk by faith, not by sight); we are of good courage, I say, and are willing rather to be absent from the body, and to be at home with the Lord. Wherefore also we make it our aim, whether at home or absent, to be well pleasing unto him. For we must all be made manifest before the judgment-seat of Christ; that each one may receive the things done in the body, according to what he hath done, whether it be good or bad" (2 Cor. 5: 1-10).

Hymn—(May be sung or read, or suitable poetry may be used instead).

Then the minister may say:

We seek comfort, let us find it in the Scriptures.

"For I am already being offered, and the time of my departure is come. I have fought the good fight, I have finished the course, I have kept the faith: henceforth there is laid up for me the crown of righteousness, which the Lord, the righteous judge, shall give to me at that day; and not to me only, but also to all them that have loved his appearing" (2 Tim. 4: 6-8).

"Wherefore girding up the loins of your mind, be sober and set your hope perfectly on the grace that is to be brought unto you at the revelation of Jesus Christ; as children of obedience, not fashioning yourselves according to your former lusts in the time of your ignorance: but like as he who called you is holy, be ye yourselves also holy in all manner of living. Because it is written, ye shall be holy; for I am holy. And if ye call on him as Father, who without respect of persons, judgeth according to each man's work, pass the time of your sojourning in fear: knowing that ye were redeemed, not with corruptible things, with silver or gold, from your vain manner of life handed down from your fathers; but with precious blood, as of a lamb without blemish and without spot, even the blood of Christ: who was foreknown indeed before the foundation of the world, but was manifested at the end of the times for your sake, who through him are believers in God, that raised him from the dead, and gave him glory; so that your faith and hope might be in God" (1 Pet. 1: 13-21).

"The hoary head is a crown of glory; it shall be found in the way of righteousness" (Prov. 16: 31).

"Hast thou not known? hast thou not heard? The everlasting God, Jehovah, the Creator of the ends of the earth, fainteth not, neither is weary; there is no searching of his understanding. He giveth power to the faint; and to him that hath no might he increaseth strength. Even the youths shall faint and be weary, and the young men shall utterly fall:

but they that wait for Jehovah shall renew their strength; they shall mount up with wings as eagles; they shall run and not be weary; they shall walk and not faint" (Isa. 40: 28-31).

"Remember also thy Creator in the days of thy youth, before the evil days come, and the years draw nigh, when thou shalt say, I have no pleasure in them; before the sun and the light, and the moon, and the stars are darkened, and the clouds return after the rain; in the day when the keepers of the house shall tremble, and the strong men shall bow themselves and the grinders cease because they are few, and those that look out of the windows shall be darkened, and the doors shall be shut in the street; when the sound of the grinding is low, and one shall rise up at the voice of a bird, and all the daughters of music shall be brought low; yea they shall be afraid of that which is high, and terrors shall be in the way; and the almond tree shall blossom, and the grasshopper shall be a burden, and desire shall fail; because man goeth to his everlasting home, and the mourners go about the streets: before the silver cord is loosed, or the golden bowl is broken, or the pitcher is broken at the fountain, or the wheel broken at the cistern, and the dust returneth to the

earth as it was, and the spirit returneth unto
God who gave it" (Eccles. 12: 1-7).

"Lord, thou hast been our dwelling place in
all generations. Before the mountains were
brought forth, or ever thou hadst formed the
earth and the world, even from everlasting
to everlasting, thou art God. Thou turnest
man to destruction; and sayest, Return, ye
children of men. For a thousand years in
thy sight are but as yesterday when it is past,
and as a watch in the night. Thou carriest
them away as with a flood; they are as a sleep:
in the morning they are like grass which
groweth up. In the morning it flourisheth,
and groweth up; in the evening it is cut down,
and withereth. For we are consumed in thine
anger, and in thy wrath are we troubled. Thou
hast set our iniquities before thee, our secret
sins in the light of thy countenance. For all
our days are passed away in thy wrath: we
bring our years to an end as a sigh. The days
of our years are threescore years and ten, or
even by reason of strength fourscore years;
yet is their pride but labor and sorrow; for
it is soon gone, and we fly away. Who knoweth the power of thine anger, and thy wrath
according to the fear that is due unto thee?
So teach us to number our days, that we may
get us a heart of wisdom. Return, O Jehovah;

how long? And let it repent thee concerning thy servants. Oh satisfy us in the morning with thy lovingkindness, that we may rejoice and be glad all our days. Make us glad according to the days wherein thou hast afflicted us, and the years wherein we have seen evil. Let thy work appear unto thy servants, and thy glory upon their children. And let the favor of the Lord our God be upon us; and establish thou the work of our hands upon us; yea, the work of our hands establish thou it" (Psalm 90).

Then the minister may say:

Having heard God speak to us in his Word, let us now take our sorrow to him being assured that he will hear us by the following blessed words:

"Draw nigh to God, and he will draw nigh to you. Cleanse your hands, ye sinners; and purify your hearts, ye doubleminded. . . . Humble yourselves in the sight of the Lord, and he shall exalt you" (James 4: 8, 10).

Prayer.

Hymn—(May be sung or read, or suitable poetry may be used instead).

Address—(If deemed advisable).

Hymn—(May be sung or read, or suitable poetry may be used instead).

Then the minister may say:

The services here are now concluded, and we will repair to the cemetery where the interment will take place.

(Minister takes place in lead of pallbearers and walks from home or church in this order to the funeral carriage. Upon arrival at the cemetery the minister again takes his place in the lead of the pallbearers and walks in this order to the grave).

Then the minister may say (as he walks in the lead of the procession):

"And I heard a voice from heaven saying, Write, Blessed are the dead who die in the Lord from henceforth: yea, saith the Spirit, that they may rest from their labors; for their works follow with them" (Rev. 14: 13).

"Thou wilt guide me with thy counsel, and afterward receive me to glory. Whom have I in heaven but thee? And there is none upon earth that I desire besides thee. My flesh and my heart faileth; but God is the strength of my heart and my portion for ever" (Psalm 73: 24-26).

(When the casket has been placed on the supports ready for lowering into the grave, the minister takes his stand at the head of the grave).

Then the minister may say (as the casket is lowered):

"Now this I say, brethren, that flesh and blood cannot inherit the kingdom of God;

neither doth corruption inherit incorruption. Behold, I tell you a mystery: we all shall not sleep, but we shall all be changed, in a moment, in the twinkling of an eye, at the last trump: for the trumpet shall sound, and the dead shall be raised incorruptible, and we shall be changed. For this corruptible must put on incorruption, and this mortal must put on immortality. But when this corruptible shall have put on incorruption, and this mortal shall have put on immortality then shall come to pass the saying that is written, Death is swallowed up in victory. O death, where is thy victory? O death, where is thy sting? The sting of death is sin; and the power of sin is the law: but thanks be to God, who giveth us the victory through our Lord Jesus Christ. Wherefore, my beloved brethren, be ye stedfast, unmovable, always abounding in the work of the Lord, forasmuch as ye know that your labor is not vain in the Lord" (1 Cor. 15: 50-58).

Then the minister may use the following committal service:

My Friends: Whereas, death hath once more invaded our ranks and removed from the walks of life our beloved Brother ———, his soul having departed to dwell in "The

undiscovered country from whose bourn no
traveler returns," it has become our sad duty
to commit his body to the grave: Earth to
earth, ashes to ashes, dust to dust, and our inspiring privilege to commend his soul to our
Maker, Father, and Redeemer, in the confident
hope of the coming again of our Lord and
Saviour Jesus Christ, the resurrection of the
body from the grave, and the joyous life reserved for the children of light in the realms
of glory.

(Then the grave may be filled or canopied and
decorated with flowers, after which the people may
be dismissed by prayer or benediction).

Dismissing the people the minister may say:

"The peace of God, which passeth all understanding, shall guard your hearts and your
thoughts in Christ Jesus. . . . Now unto our
God and Father be the glory for ever and ever.
Amen" (Phil. 4: 7, 20).

Funeral Service for an Aged Woman or Mother

OPENING:

The minister may say:

"Then shall the King say unto them on his right hand, Come, ye blessed of my Father, inherit the kingdom prepared for you from the foundation of the world: for I was hungry, and ye gave me to eat; I was thirsty and ye gave me drink; I was a stranger and ye took me in; naked, and ye clothed me; I was sick, and ye visited me; I was in prison, and ye came unto me. Then shall the righteous answer him saying, Lord, when saw we thee hungry, and fed thee? or athirst, and gave thee drink? And when saw we thee a stranger, and took thee in? or naked, and clothed thee? And when saw we thee sick, or in prison, and came unto thee? And the King shall answer and say unto them, Verily I say unto you, Inasmuch as ye did it unto one of these my brethren, even these least, ye did it unto me" (Matt. 25: 34-40).

Hymn—(May be sung **or read**, or **suitable** poetry may be used instead).

Then the minister may say:

Beloved, let us seek comfort in the Word of God, giving heed to the Bible description of a good woman:

"A worthy woman who can find? For her price is far above rubies. The heart of her husband trusteth in her, and he shall have no lack of gain. She doeth him good and not evil all the days of her life. She seeketh wool and flax, and worketh willingly with her hands. She is like the merchant-ships; she bringeth her bread from afar. She riseth also while it is yet night, and giveth food to her household, and their task to her maidens. She considereth a field, and buyeth it; with the fruit of her hands she planteth a vineyard. She girdeth her loins with strength and maketh strong her arms. She perceiveth that her merchandise is profitable; her lamp goeth not out by night. She layeth her hands to the distaff, and her hands hold the spindle. She stretcheth out her hand to the poor; yea, she reacheth forth her hands to the needy. She is not afraid of the snow for her household; for all her household are clothed with scarlet. She maketh for herself carpets of tapestry; her clothing is fine linen and purple. Her husband is known in the gates, when he sitteth among the elders of the land. She maketh

linen garments and selleth them, and deliver-
eth girdles unto the merchant. Strength and
dignity are her clothing; and she laugheth
at the time to come. She openeth her mouth
with wisdom; and the law of kindness is on
her tongue. She looketh well to the ways of
her household, and eateth not the bread of
idleness. Her children rise up and call her
blessed; her husband also, and he praiseth
her, saying: Many daughters have done worth-
ily, but thou excellest them all. Grace is de-
ceitful, and beauty is vain, but a woman that
feareth Jehovah, she shall be praised" (Prov.
31: 10-30).

If we would be comforted in the Word of
God's care for his own, let us heed:

"Behold, happy is the man whom God correcteth; therefore despise not thou the chastening of the Almighty. For he maketh sore,
and bindeth up; he woundeth, and his hands
make whole. He will deliver thee in six
troubles; yea, in seven there shall no evil
touch thee. In famine he will redeem thee
from death; and in war from the power of the
sword. Thou shalt be hid from the scourge
of the tongue: neither shalt thou be afraid of
destruction when it cometh. At destruction
and dearth thou shalt laugh; neither shalt
thou be afraid of the beasts of the earth. For

thou shalt be in league with the stones of the field; and the beasts of the field shall be at peace with thee. And thou shalt know that thy tent is in peace; and thou shalt visit thy fold, and shalt miss nothing. Thou shalt know also that thy seed shall be great, and thine offspring as the grass of the earth. Thou shalt come to thy grave in a full age, like as a shock of grain cometh in its season" (Job 5: 17-26).

If we would be comforted in the thought of the future of God's saints, let us heed:

"And I saw a new heaven and a new earth: for the first heaven and the first earth are passed away; and the sea is no more. And I saw the holy city, new Jerusalem, coming down out of heaven from God, made ready as a bride adorned for her husband. And I heard a great voice out of the throne saying, Behold, the tabernacle of God is with men, and he shall dwell with them, and they shall be his peoples, and God himself shall be with them, and be their God: and he shall wipe away every tear from their eyes; and death shall be no more; neither shall there be mourning, nor crying, nor pain, any more: the first things are passed away. And he that sitteth on the throne said, Behold, I make all things new. And he saith, Write: for these words are faithful and true. And he said unto me, They are come to pass. I am the Alpha and the Omega the beginning and the end. I will give unto him that is athirst of the fountain of the water of life freely. He that overcometh shall inherit these things; and I will be his God, and he shall be my son" (Rev. 21: 1-7).

Then the minister may say:

Having heard God speaking to us in his Word, let us now take our sorrow to him, being assured that he will hear us by the following blessed words:

"Draw nigh to God, and he will draw nigh to you. Cleanse your hands, ye sinners; and purify your hearts, ye doubleminded. . . . Humble yourselves in the sight of the Lord, and he shall exalt you" (James 4: 8, 10).

Prayer.

Hymn—(May be sung or read, or suitable poetry may be used instead).

Address—(If deemed advisable).

Hymn—(May be sung or read, or suitable poetry may be used instead).

Then the minister may say:

The services here are now concluded, and we will repair to the cemetery where the interment will take place.

(Minister takes place in lead of pallbearers and walks from home or church in this order to the funeral carriage. Upon arrival at the cemetery the minister again takes his place in the lead of the pallbearers and walks in this order to the grave).

Then the minister may say (as he walks in the lead of the procession):

"And I heard a voice from heaven saying, Write, Blessed are the dead who die in the Lord from henceforth: yea, saith the Spirit, that they may rest from their labors; for their works follow with them" (Rev. 14: 13).

"Thou wilt guide me with thy counsel, and afterward receive me to glory. Whom have I in heaven but thee? And there is none upon earth that I desire besides thee. My flesh and my heart faileth; but God is the strength of my heart and my portion for ever" (Psalm 73: 24-26).

(When the casket has been placed on the supports ready for lowering into the grave, the minister takes his stand at the head of the grave).

Then the minister may say (as the casket is lowered):

"Now this I say, brethren, that flesh and blood cannot inherit the kingdom of God; neither doth corruption inherit incorruption. Behold, I tell you a mystery: we all shall not sleep, but we shall all be changed, in a moment, in the twinkling of an eye, at the last trump: for the trumpet shall sound, and the dead shall be raised incorruptible, and we shall be changed. For this corruptible must put on incorruption, and this mortal must put on immortality. But when this corruptible shall have put on incorruption, and this mortal shall have put on immortality, then shall come to pass the saying that is written, Death is swallowed up in victory. O death, where is thy victory? O death, where is thy sting? The sting of death is sin; and the power of sin is the law: but thanks be to God, who giveth us the victory through our Lord Jesus Christ. Wherefore, my beloved brethren, be ye stedfast, unmovable, always abounding in the work of the Lord, forasmuch as ye know that your labor is not vain in the Lord" (1 Cor. 15: 50-58).

Then the minister may use the following committal service:

My Friends: Whereas, death hath once more invaded our ranks and removed from the walks of life our beloved Sister ———, her soul having departed to dwell in "The undiscovered country from whose bourn no traveler returns," it has become our sad duty to commit her body to the grave: Earth to earth, ashes to ashes, dust to dust, and our inspiring privilege to commend her soul to our Maker, Father, and Redeemer, in the confident hope of the coming again of our Lord and Saviour Jesus Christ, the resurrection of the body from the grave, and the joyous life reserved for the children of light in the realms of glory.

(Then the grave may be filled or canopied and decorated with flowers, after which the people may be dismissed by prayer or benediction).

Dismissing the people the minister may say:

"The peace of God, which passeth all understanding, shall guard your hearts and your thoughts in Christ Jesus. . . . Now unto our God and Father be the glory for ever and ever. Amen" (Phil. 4: 7, 20).

Funeral Service for Non-Christian

OPENING:

The minister may say:

"Come unto me, all ye that labor and are heavy laden, and I will give you rest. Take my yoke upon you, and learn of me; for I am meek and lowly in heart: and ye shall find rest unto your souls" (Matt. 11: 28-29).

"None of his transgressions that he hath committed shall be remembered against him: in his righteousness that he hath done he shall live" (Ezek. 18: 22).

"And thou, son of man, say unto the house of Israel: thus ye speak, saying, Our transgressions and our sins are upon us, and we pine away in them; how then can we live? Say unto them, As I live, saith the Lord Jehovah, I have no pleasure in the death of the wicked; but that the wicked turn from his way and live: turn ye, turn ye from your evil ways; for why will ye die, O house of Israel?" (Ezek. 33: 10, 11).

"Now on the last day, the great day of the feast, Jesus stood and cried, saying, If any

man thirst, let him come unto me and drink"
(John 7: 37).

Hymn—(May be sung or read, or suitable
poetry may be used instead).

Then the minister may say:

The Word of God abounds in hope, inspiring instructions regarding eternal life and
how to obtain it.   Hear how Jesus saved a
condemned man:

"And one of the malefactors that were
hanged railed on him, saying, Art not thou
the Christ? save thyself and us.   But the
other answered, and rebuking him said, Dost
thou not even fear God, seeing thou art in
the same condemnation?   And we indeed
justly; for we receive the due reward of our
deeds: but this man hath done nothing amiss.
And he said, Jesus, remember me when thou
comest in thy kingdom.   And he said unto
him, Verily I say unto thee, To-day shalt thou
be with me in paradise" (Luke 23: 39-43).

Hear what Jesus taught a great lawyer
about salvation:

"Now there was a man of the Pharisees,
named Nicodemus, a ruler of the Jews: the
same came unto him by night, and said to him,
Rabbi, we know that thou art a teacher come
from God; for no one can do these signs that

thou doest, except God be with him.   Jesus
answered and said unto him, Verily, verily,
I say unto thee, Except one be born anew, he
cannot see the kingdom of God.   Nicodemus
saith unto him, How can a man be born when
he is old? can he enter a second time into his
mother's womb, and be born?   Jesus answered, Verily, verily, I say unto thee, Except
one be born of water and the Spirit, he cannot
enter into the kingdom of God.   That which
is born of the flesh is flesh; and that which is
born of the Spirit is spirit.   Marvel not that
I said unto thee, Ye must be born anew.   The
wind bloweth where it will, and thou hearest
the voice thereof, but knowest not whence it
cometh, and whither it goeth: so is every one
that is born of the Spirit.   Nicodemus answered and said unto him, How can these
things be?   Jesus answered and said unto
him, Art thou the teacher of Israel, and understandest not these things?   Verily, verily,
I say unto thee, We speak that which we know,
and bear witness of that which we have seen;
and ye receive not our witness.   If I told you
earthly things and ye believe not, how shall
ye believe if I tell you heavenly things?   And
no one hath ascended into heaven, but he that
descended out of heaven, even the Son of man,
who is in heaven.   And as Moses lifted up

the serpent in the wilderness, even so must the Son of man be lifted up; that whosoever believeth may in him have eternal life. For God so loved the world, that he gave his only begotten Son, that whosoever believeth on him should not perish, but have eternal life" (John 3: 1-16).

Hear what Jesus said to the rich young ruler:

"And a certain ruler asked him, saying, Good Teacher, what shall I do to inherit eternal life. And Jesus said unto him, why callest thou me good? none is good, save one, even God. Thou knowest the commandments, Do not commit adultery, Do not kill, Do not steal, Do not bear false witness, honor thy father and mother. And he said, All these things have I observed from my youth up. And when Jesus heard it, he said unto him, One thing thou lackest yet: sell all that thou hast, and distribute unto the poor, and thou shalt have treasure in heaven: and come follow me. But when he heard these things, he became exceeding sorrowful; for he was very rich. And Jesus seeing him said, How hardly shall they that have riches enter into the kingdom of God! For it is easier for a camel to enter in through a needle's eye, than for a rich man to enter into the kingdom of God. And they that heard

it said, Then who can be saved?   But he said,
The things which are impossible with men are
possible with God.   And Peter said, Lo, we
have left our own, and followed thee.   And
he said unto them, Verily I say unto you, There
is no man that hath left house, or wife, or
brethren, or parents, or children, for the kingdom of God's sake, who shall not receive mani-
fold more in this time, and in the world to
come eternal life" (Luke 18: 18-30).

And, finally, do hear that most precious and
beautiful of parables:

"And he said, A certain man had two sons:
and the younger of them said to his father,
Father, give me the portion of thy substance
that falleth to me.   And he divided unto them
his living.   And not many days after, the
younger son gathered all together and took
his journey into a far country; and there he
wasted his substance with riotous living.   And
when he had spent all, there arose a mighty
famine in that country; and he began to be
in want.   And he went and joined himself to
one of the citizens of that country; and he
sent him into his fields to feed swine.   And
he would fain have filled his belly with the
husks that the swine did eat: and no man gave
unto him.   But when he came to himself he
said, How many hired servants of my father's

have bread enough and to spare, and I perish here with hunger! I will arise and go to my father, and will say unto him, Father, I have sinned against heaven, and in thy sight: I am no more worthy to be called thy son: make me as one of thy hired servants. And he arose and came to his father. But while he was yet afar off, his father saw him, and was moved with compassion, and ran, and fell on his neck, and kissed him. And the son said unto him, Father, I have sinned against heaven, and in thy sight: I am no more worthy to be called thy son. But the father said to his servants, Bring forth quickly the best robe, and put it on him; and put a ring on his hand, and shoes on his feet: and bring the fatted calf, and kill it, and let us eat, and make merry: for this my son was dead, and is alive again; he was lost, and is found. And they began to be merry. Now his elder son was in the field: and as he came and drew nigh to the house, he heard music and dancing. And he called to him one of the servants, and inquired what these things might be. And he said unto him, Thy brother is come; and thy father hath killed the fatted calf, because he hath received him safe and sound. But he was angry, and would not go in; and his father came out, and entreated him. But he answered and said to his father, Lo, these many years do I serve thee, and I never transgressed a commandment of thine; and yet thou never gavest me a kid, that I might make merry with my friends: but when this thy son came, who hath devoured thy living with harlots, thou killedst for him the fatted calf. And he said unto him, Son, thou art ever with me, and all that is mine is thine. But it was meet to make merry and be glad: for this thy brother was dead, and is alive again; and was lost, and is found" (Luke 15: 11-32).

Then the minister may say:

Having heard the precious instruction of God's Word, let us address God in the voice of supplication in the following promise:

"Draw nigh to God, and he will draw nigh to you. Cleanse your hands, ye sinners; and purify your hearts, ye doubleminded. . . . Humble yourselves in the sight of the Lord, and he shall exalt you" (James 4: 8 10).

Prayer.

Hymn—(May be sung or read, or suitable poetry may be used instead).

Address—(If deemed advisable).

Hymn—(May be sung or read, or suitable poetry may be used instead).

Then the minister may say:

The services here are now concluded, and we will repair to the cemetery where the interment will take place.

(Minister takes place in lead of pallbearers and walks from home or church in this order to the funeral carriage. Upon arrival at the cemetery the minister again takes his place in the lead of the pallbearers and walks in this order to the grave).

Then the minister may say (as he walks in the lead of the procession):

"Seek ye Jehovah while he may be found; call ye upon him while he is near: let the wicked forsake his way, and the unrighteous man his thoughts; and let him return unto Jehovah, and he will have mercy upon him; and to our God, for he will abundantly pardon" (Isa. 55: 6, 7).

"Hearken to me, ye that follow after righteousness, ye that seek Jehovah: look unto the rock whence ye were hewn, and to the hole of the pit whence ye were digged. Look unto Abraham your father, and unto Sarah that bare you; for when he was but one I called him, and I blessed him, and made him many. For Jehovah hath comforted Zion; he hath comforted all her waste places, and hath made her wilderness like Eden, and her desert like the garden of Jehovah; joy and gladness shall be found therein, thanksgiving, and the voice of melody" (Isa. 51: 1-3).

"And the Spirit and the bride say, Come. And he that heareth, let him say, Come. And he that is athirst, let him come: he that will, let him take the water of life freely" (Rev. 22: 17).

(When the casket has been placed on the supports ready for lowering into the grave, the minister takes his stand at the head of the grave).

Then the minister may say (as the casket is lowered):

"But we would not have you ignorant, brethren, concerning them that fall asleep; that ye sorrow not, even as the rest, who have no hope. For if we believe that Jesus died and rose again, even so them also that are fallen asleep in Jesus will God bring with him. For this we say unto you by the word of the Lord, that we that are alive, that are left unto the coming of the Lord, shall in no wise precede them that are fallen asleep. For the Lord himself shall descend from heaven, with a shout, with the voice of the archangel, and with the trump of God: and the dead in Christ shall rise first; then we that are alive, that are left, shall together with them be caught up in the clouds, to meet the Lord in the air: and so shall we

ever be with the Lord.   Wherefore comfort
one another with these words" (1 Thess. 4:
13-18).

Then the minister may use the following committal service:

My Friends: Whereas, death hath once
more invaded our ranks and removed from
the walks of life our beloved Brother (or
Sister)——————, his (or her) soul having
departed to dwell in "The undiscovered country from whose bourn no traveler returns,"
it has become our sad duty to commit his
(or her) body to the grave: Earth to earth,
ashes to ashes, dust to dust, and our inspiring
privilege to commend his (or her) soul to our
Maker, Father, and Redeemer, in the confident
hope of the coming again of our Lord and
Saviour Jesus Christ, the resurrection of the
body from the grave, and the joyous life reserved for the children of light in the realms
of glory.

(Then the grave may be filled or canopied and
decorated with flowers, after which the people may
be dismissed by prayer or benediction).

Dismissing the people the minister may say:

"The peace of God, which passeth all understanding, shall guard your hearts and your
thoughts in Christ Jesus. . . . Now unto our
God and Father be the glory for ever and ever.
Amen" (Phil. 4: 7, 20).

The Funeral Service of the Protestant Episcopal Church

Abbreviated, and in general use by Methodist, Presbyterian, Baptist, and other churches

The minister, meeting the corpse and going before it, shall say:

"I am the resurrection and the life, saith the Lord: he that believeth in me, though he were dead, yet shall he live; and whosoever liveth and believeth in me, shall never die.

"I know that my Redeemer liveth, and that he shall stand at the latter day upon the earth. And though, after my skin, worms destroy this body, yet in my flesh shall I see God; whom I shall see for myself and mine eyes shall behold and not another.

"We brought nothing into this world, and it is certain we can carry nothing out. The Lord gave and the Lord hath taken away; blessed be the name of the Lord."

Then shall be said or sung the following anthem:

"Lord make me to know my end, and the number of my days; that I may be certified how long I have to live. Behold, thou hast made my days as it were a span long, and mine age is even as nothing in respect of thee; and verily every man living is altogether vanity.

For man walketh in a vain shadow, and disquieteth himself in vain: he heapeth up riches and cannot tell who shall gather them.

And now Lord what is my hope? Truly my hope is even in thee.

I am a stranger with thee and a sojourner as all my fathers were.

Lord, thou hast been our refuge from one generation to another.

Before the mountains were brought forth, or even the earth or the world was made, thou art God from everlasting, and world without end.

Thou turnest man to destruction; again thou sayest, come again, ye children of men.

For a thousand years in thy sight are but as yesterday, seeing that is past as a watch in the night.

The days of our age are threescore years and ten, and though men be so strong that they come to fourscore years, yet is their strength then but labor and sorrow and we are gone.

So teach us to number our days, that we may apply our hearts unto wisdom.

Glory be to the Father, and to the Son, and to the Holy Ghost; and as it was in the beginning, is now, and ever shall be, world without end. Amen."

Then shall follow this lesson:

"Now is Christ risen from the dead, and become the first fruits of them that slept. For since by man came death, by man came also the resurrection of the dead. For as in Adam all die, even so in Christ shall all be made alive. But every man in his own order: Christ the first-fruits; afterward they that are Christ's at his coming. Then cometh the end, when he shall have delivered up the kingdom to God, even the Father; when he shall have put down all rule, and all authority, and power. For he must reign, till he hath put all enemies under his feet. The last enemy that shall be destroyed is death. For he hath put all things under his feet.

But some man will say, How are the dead raised up? and with what body do they come? Thou fool! that which thou sowest is not quickened, except it die. And that which thou sowest, thou sowest not that body that shall be, but bare grain, it may chance of wheat, or of some other grain. But God giveth it a body as it hath pleased him, and to every seed his own body.

Now this I say, brethren, that flesh and blood cannot inherit the kingdom of God; neither doth corruption inherit incorruption.

Behold, I show you a mystery; we shall not all sleep, but we shall all be changed. In a moment, in the twinkling of an eye, at the last trump, for the trumpet shall sound, and the dead shall be raised incorruptible, and we shall be changed.

For this corruptible must put on incorruption, and this mortal must put on immortality.

So when this corruptible shall have put on incorruption, and this mortal shall have put on immortality, then shall be brought to pass the saying that is written, death is swallowed up in victory.

O death, where is thy sting? O grave, where is thy victory?

The sting of death is sin; and the strength of sin is the law.

But thanks be to God, which giveth us the victory through our Lord Jesus Christ.

Therefore, my beloved brethren, be ye steadfast, unmovable, always abounding in the work of the Lord, forasmuch as ye know that your labor is not in vain in the Lord."

When they come to the grave, while the corpse is made ready to be laid into the earth, shall be sung or said:

"Man, that is born of woman, hath but a short time to live, and is full of misery. He cometh up and is cut down, like a flower; he fleeth as it were a shadow, and never continueth in one stay.

In the midst of life we are in death: of whom may we seek for succor, but of thee, O Lord, who for our sins art justly displeased?

Thou knowest, Lord, the secrets of our hearts; shut not thy merciful ears to our prayer; but spare us, Lord most holy, O God most mighty, O holy and merciful Saviour, thou most worthy Judge eternal; suffer us not, at our last hour, for any pains of death, to fall from thee."

Then while the earth shall be cast upon the body by some standing by, the minister shall say:

Forasmuch as it hath pleased Almighty God, in his wise providence, to take out of this world the soul of our deceased brother, we therefore commit his body to the ground; earth to earth; ashes to ashes, dust to dust; looking for the general resurrection in the last day, and the life of the world to come, through our Lord Jesus Christ; at whose sec-

ond coming in glorious majesty to judge the
world, the earth and the sea shall give up
their dead; and the corruptible bodies of those
who sleep in him shall be changed, and made
like unto his own glorious body; according to
the mighty working whereby he is able to sub-
due all things unto himself.

Then shall be said or sung:

"I heard a voice from heaven, saying unto
me, write, from henceforth, blessed are the
dead who die in the Lord: even so, saith the
Spirit, for they rest from their labors."

Then the minister shall say the following prayer:

Almighty God, with whom do live the spir-
its of those who depart hence in the Lord, and
with whom the souls of the faithful, after they
are delivered from the burden of the flesh,
are in joy and felicity; we give thee hearty
thanks for the good examples of all those thy
servants, who, having finished their course in
faith, do now rest from their labors.   And we
beseech thee, that we, with all those who are
departed in the true faith of thy holy Name,
may have our perfect consummation and bliss,
both in body and soul, in thy eternal and everlasting glory; through Jesus Christ our Lord.
Amen.

The grace of our Lord Jesus Christ, and the love of God, and the fellowship of the Holy Ghost, be with us all evermore. Amen.

Texts for Funeral Addresses

1 Cor. 13: 12: "For now we see in a mirror, darkly; but then face to face: now I know in part; but then shall I know fully even as also I was fully known."

James 4: 14: "Whereas ye know not what shall be on the morrow. What is your life? For ye are a vapor that appeareth for a little time, and then vanisheth away."

Psalm 17: 15: "As for me, I shall behold thy face in righteousness; I shall be satisfied, when I awake, with beholding thy form."

Psalm 116: 15: "Precious in the sight of Jehovah is the death of his saints."

Rev. 20: 11-13: "And I saw a great white throne, and him that sat upon it, from whose face the earth and the heaven fled away; and there was found no place for them. And I saw the dead, the great and the small, standing before the throne; and books were opened: and another book was opened, which is the book of life: and the dead were judged out of the things which were written in the books, according to their works. And the sea gave up the dead that were in it; and death and Hades gave up the dead that were in them: and they were judged every man according to their works."

John 14: 2: "In my Father's house are many mansions; if it were not so, I would have told you; for I go to prepare a place for you."

Heb. 9: 27: "And inasmuch as it is appointed unto men once to die, and after this cometh judgment."

Phil. 1: 23: "But I am in a strait betwixt the two, having the desire to depart and be with Christ; for it is very far better."

1 Cor. 15: 26: "The last enemy that shall be abolished is death."

Eccl. 9: 5: "For the living know that they shall die: but the dead know not anything, neither have they any more a reward; for the memory of them is forgotten."

Isa. 61: 1: "The Spirit of the Lord Jehovah is upon me; because Jehovah hath anointed me to preach good tidings unto the meek; he hath sent me to bind up the broken-hearted, to proclaim liberty to the captives, and the opening of the prison to them that are bound."

2 Cor. 1: 3, 4: "Blessed be the God and Father of our Lord Jesus Christ, the Father

of mercies and God of all comfort; who comforteth us in all our affliction, that we may be able to comfort them that are in any affliction, through the comfort wherewith we ourselves are comforted of God."

2 Tim. 1: 10: "But hath now been manifested by the appearing of our Saviour Christ Jesus, who abolished death, and brought life and immortality to light through the gospel."

Job 14: 14: "If a man die, shall he live again? All the days of my warfare would I wait, till my release should come."

John 10: 10: "The thief cometh not, but that he may steal, and kill, and destroy: I came that they may have life, and may have it abundantly."

Heb. 10: 16: "This is the covenant that I will make with them after those days, saith the Lord: I will put my laws on their heart, and upon their mind also will I write them."

2 Cor. 5: 5: "Now he that wrought us for this very thing is God, who gave unto us the earnest of the Spirit."

Psalm 90: 12: "So teach us to number our days, that we may get us a heart of wisdom."

John 1: 4: "In him was life; and the life was the light of men."

Matt. 28: 6: "He is not here; for he is risen, even as he said. Come, see the place where the Lord lay."

Numbers 23: 10: "Who can count the dust of Jacob, or number the fourth part of Israel? Let me die the death of the righteous and let my last end be like his!"

Rev. 21: 4: "And he shall wipe away every tear from their eyes; and death shall be no more; neither shall there be mourning, nor crying, nor pain, any more: the first things are passed away."

Phil. 4: 13: "I can do all things in him that strengtheneth me."

Psalm 27: 5: "For in the day of trouble he will keep me secretly in his pavilion; in the covert of his tabernacle will he hide me; he will lift me up upon a rock."

Isa. 40: 11: "He will feed his flock like a shepherd, he will gather the lambs in his arm, and carry them in his bosom, and will gently lead those that have their young."

1 Cor. 15: 58: "Wherefore, my beloved brethren, be ye stedfast, unmovable, always abounding in the work of the Lord, forasmuch as ye know that your labor is not vain in the Lord."

1 John 5: 4: "For whatsoever is begotten of God overcometh the world: and this is the

victory that hath overcome the world, even our faith."

Amos 5: 8: "Seek him that maketh the Pleiades and Orion, and turneth the shadow of death into the morning, and maketh the day dark with night; that calleth for the waters of the sea, and poureth them out upon the face of the earth (Jehovah is his name)."

Psalm 88: 18: "Lover and friend hast thou put far from me, and mine acquaintance into darkness."

1 Thess. 4: 13: "But we would not have you ignorant, brethren, concerning them that fall asleep; that ye sorrow not, even as the rest, who have no hope."

Phil. 3: 20, 21: "For our citizenship is in heaven; whence also we wait for a Saviour, the Lord Jesus Christ: who shall fashion anew the body of our humiliation, that it may be conformed to the body of his glory, according to the working whereby he is able even to subject all things unto himself."

1 Cor. 15: 49: "And as we have borne the image of the earthy, we shall also bear the image of the heavenly."

1 Cor. 2: 9, 10: "But as it is written, things which eye saw not, and ear heard not, and which entered not into the heart of man, whatsoever things God prepared for them that love

him. But unto us God revealed them through the Spirit: for the Spirit searcheth all things, yea the deep things of God."

Matt. 25: 34: "Then shall the King say unto them on his right hand, Come, ye blessed of my Father, inherit the kingdom prepared for you from the foundation of the world."

Rev. 14: 13: "And I heard a voice from heaven saying, Write, Blessed are the dead who die in the Lord from henceforth: yea, saith the Spirit, that they may rest from their labors; for their works follow with them."

Rev. 7: 14: "And I say unto him, My Lord, thou knowest. And he said to me, These are they that come out of the great tribulation, and they washed their robes, and made them white in the blood of the Lamb."

Heb. 12: 5, 6: "And ye have forgotten the exhortation which reasoneth with you as with sons. My son, regard not lightly the chastening of the Lord, nor faint when thou art reproved of him; for whom the Lord loveth he chasteneth, and scourgeth every son whom he receiveth."

Psalm 23: 4: "Yea, though I walk through the valley of the shadow of death, I will fear no evil; for thou art with me; thy rod and thy staff they comfort me."

Matt. 19: 14: "But Jesus said, Suffer the little children, and forbid them not to come unto me: for to such belongeth the kingdom of heaven."

Mark 10: 14: "But when Jesus saw it, he was moved with indignation, and said unto them, Suffer the little children to come unto me; forbid them not: for to such belongeth the kingdom of God."

2 Sam. 12: 23: "But now he is dead, wherefore should I fast? Can I bring him back again? I shall go to him, but he will not return to me."

Luke 8: 52: "And all were weeping and bewailing her: but he said, Weep not; for she is not dead, but sleepeth."

Psalm 37: 37: "Mark the perfect man, and behold the upright; for there is a happy end to the man of peace."

2 Cor. 5: 1: "For we know that if the earthly house of our tabernacle be dissolved, we have a building from God, a house not made with hands, eternal, in the heavens."

Poetry

General

THERE IS NO DEATH

There is no death! The stars go down
  To rise upon some other shore,
And bright in Heaven's jeweled crown
  They shine for evermore.

There is no death! An angel form
  Walks o'er the earth with silent tread;
He bears our best loved things away,
  And then we call them "dead."

He leaves our hearts all desolate;
  He plucks our fairest, sweetest flowers;
Transplanted into bliss, they now
  Adorn immortal bowers.
                    —*John L. McCreery.*

๙ ๙

CROSSING THE BAR

Sunset and evening star,
  And one clear call for me!
And may there be no moaning at the bar
  When I put out to sea.

But such a tide as moving seems asleep,
    Too full for sound and foam,
When that which drew from out the boundless
    deep,
    Turns again home.

Twilight and evening bell,
    And after that the dark!
And may there be no sadness of farewell
    When I embark.

For though from out our bourne of Time and
    Place,
    The flood may bear me far,
I hope to see my Pilot face to face,
    When I have crossed the bar.

—*Tennyson.*

    ❧ ❧

THE HOLY SPRINGTIME

The flowers that bloom through the summer,
    In the autumn will be dead;
And all winter long 'neath the cover of snow
    Their beauty will be hid.
But when the bright springtime comes,
    To waken them from their sleep,
Their hidden beauty again will appear.
    Their soft petals again will be sweet.

So it is with the people:
    For when God sees best,
After their summer of ceaseless bloom,
    He will give them a winter's rest.
He will cause the autumn winds
    To make them droop and die;
And we will long for those beautiful flowers,
    As the winter days go by.

But the springtime, too, will come to them,
  And God will waken them all;
O, then, how pure and sweet and holy,
  They will bloom to answer his call!
God will be the Gardener,
  In that Great Garden of Flowers,
And all the time of eternity
  Will be filled with bright springtime hours.
                    —*Grace Welker Dowling.*

SOME OF THESE DAYS

Some of these days all the skies will be brighter;
Some of these days all burdens will be lighter;
Hearts will be happier, souls will be whiter,
      Some of these days!

Some of these days, in the deserts upspringing,
Fountains shall flash while the joy-bells are ring-
    ing;
And the world—with its sweetest of words—shall
    go singing,
      Some of these days!

Some of these days! Let us bear with our sorrow!
Faith in the future—its light we may borrow;
There will be joy in the golden tomorrow —
      Some of these days!
                    —*Frank L. Stanton.*

SONG OF IMMORTALITY

Arise, arise! O Soul, and sing!
  The Lord of Life hath come in might;
And all the world is blossoming
  Beneath his kiss of love and light!

The hills doff robes of rusty brown,
   And, draped in living tapestries,
With sunshine for a golden crown,
   Return the smiles of cloudless skies.

The air is full of winged delight,
   A-thrill with joy the dullest clod,
The trees, all hung with garlands white,
   Breathe smokeless incense unto God.

And thou, O Soul, with eyes to see,
   And ears that like fine harps are strung,
With heart that thrones Divinity
   And knows Love's universal tongue,

Shouldst voice a rapture all divine,
   And fair as any flower be
The garments that about thee shine,
   Thou heir of immortality!
            —*Elizabeth Loe Watson.*

FRIEND AFTER FRIEND DEPARTS

Friend after friend departs;
   Who hath not lost a friend?
There is no union here of hearts,
   That finds not here an end;
Were this frail world our only rest,
Living or dying, none were blest.

Beyond the flight of time,
   Beyond this vale of death
There surely is some blessed clime
   Where life is not a breath,
Nor life's affection transient fire,
Whose sparks fly upward to expire.

There is a world above,
  Where parting is unknown;
A whole eternity of love,
  Formed for the good alone;
And faith beholds the dying here,
Translated to that happier sphere.

Thus star by star declines,
  Till all are passed away,
As morning high and higher shines,
  To pure and perfect day;
Nor sink those stars in empty night;
They hide themselves in heaven's own
    light.

    —*James Montgomery.*

ঃ ঃ

BLESSED ARE THEY THAT MOURN

Oh, deem not they are blest alone,
  Whose lives a peaceful tenor keep;
The power who pities man, has shown
  A blessing for the eyes that weep.

The light of smiles shall fill again
  The lids that overflow with tears;
And weary hours of woe and pain
  Are promises of happier years.

There is a day of sunny rest
  For every dark and troubled night;
And grief may bide an evening guest,
  But joy shall come with early light.

And thou who o'er thy friend's low bier
  Dost shed the bitter drops like rain,
Hope that a brighter, happier sphere
  Will give him to thy arms again.

Now let the good man's trust depart,
  Though life its common gifts deny—
Though with a pierced and bleeding heart;
  And spurned of men, he goes to die.

For God hath marked each sorrowing day
  And numbered every secret tear,
And heaven's long age of bliss shall pay
  For all his children suffer here.
          —*William Cullen Bryant.*

જ્ર જ્ર

MY DEAD

I cannot think of them as dead
  Who walk with me no more;
Along the path of life I tread
  They have but gone before.

The Father's house is mansioned fair
  Beyond my vision dim;
All souls are his, and here or there
  Are living unto him.

And still their silent ministry
  Within my heart hath place,
As when on earth they walked with me
  And met me face to face.

Their lives are made forever mine;
  What they to me have been
Hath left henceforth its seal and sign
  Engraven deep within.

Mine are they by an ownership
  Nor time nor death can free;
For God hath given to Love to keep
  Its own eternally.
                    —*Frederick L. Hosmer.*

❧ ❧

I WOULD NOT GRIEVE TOO MUCH

I would not grieve too much. The promise tells
  That rest is his who sleeps so sweetly there;
Beyond the dull, slow tolling of the bells
  Which marks his passing, life is free from care.

You would not mourn if one you love should rise
  To wear the royal purple and the crown.
Should gain the glory of the great wise
  And put the tools of humble service down.

Suppose that life should call some friend you know
  Out of the ranks, and end his days of care,
You would rejoice and smile to see him go,
  Though you remained to work and struggle there

Should high promotion call some friend away
  To crown with conquest all his earthly years,
You would not plead and beg with him to stay,
  But, thinking of his joy, you'd hide your tears.

So when death comes, though hard it seems to bear
   And long the years with all their loneliness,
The loved one has been called away from care
   To high promotion, rest and happiness.

He has been called from pain and hurt and strife,
   From all the ills which fall to flesh and clay,
He has been raised unto an ampler life.
   Nor should we mourn too much who still must
      stay.

                  —*Edgar A. Guest.*

        * *

Child

THE ETERNAL GOODNESS

I long for household voices fond,
   For vanished smiles I long
But God hath led my dear ones on,
   And he can do no wrong.

I know not what the future hath
   Of marvel or surprise,
Assured alone that life and death
   His mercy underlies.

And if my heart and flesh are weak
   To bear an untried pain,
The bruised reed he will not break,
   But strengthen and sustain.

And so beside the Silent Sea
   I wait the muffled oar;
No harm from him can come to me
   On ocean and on shore.

I know not where his islands lift
  Their fronded palms in air;
I only know I cannot drift
  Beyond his love and care.
                    —*John Greenleaf Whittier.*

⚜ ⚜

GOD KNOWS AND CARES

Men send their ships, the eager things,
  To try their luck at sea;
But none can tell by note or count
  How many there may be.
One turneth east, another south,
  They never come again,
And then we know they must have sunk,
  But neither how nor when.

God sends his happy birds abroad;
  "They're less than ships," say we;
No moment passes but he knows
  How many there should be.
One buildeth high, another low,
  With just a bird's light care;
If only one, perchance doth fall,
  God knoweth when and where.

                                —*Anon.*

⚜ ⚜

WHATEVER IS—IS BEST

I know as my life grows older,
  And mine eyes have clearer sight—
That under each rank wrong, somewhere
  There lies the root of Right;
That each sorrow has it purpose,
  By the sorrowing oft unguessed,
But as sure as the sun brings the morning,
  Whatever is—is best.

I know that each sinful action,
  As sure as the night brings shade,
Is somewhere, sometime punished,
  Tho' the hour be long delayed.
I know that the soul is aided
  Sometime by the heart's unrest,
And to grow means often to suffer—
  But whatever is—is best.
                    —*Ella Wheeler Wilcox.*

              ᴖ ᴖ

Young Man

THE FREEDOM OF DEATH

Fear no more the heat o' the sun,
  Nor the furious winter's rages;
Thou thy worldly task hast done,
  Home art gone and ta'en thy wages:
Golden lads and girls all must,
As chimney-sweepers, come to dust.

Fear no more frown o' the great,
  Thou art past the tyrant's stroke;
Care no more to clothe and eat;
  To thee the reed is as the oak:
The scepter, learning, physic, must
All follow this and come to dust.

Fear no more the lightning-flash,
  Nor the all-dreaded thunder-stone;
Fear no slander, censure rash;
  Thou hast finished joy and moan;
All lovers young, all lovers must
Consign to thee, and come to dust.

No exorciser harm thee!
Nor no witchcraft charm thee!
Ghost unlaid forbear thee!
Nothing ill come near thee!
Quiet consummation have;
And renowned be thy grave!

—*Shakespeare.*

❧ ❧

A MAN OF GOD

Clothe me in the rose tints of thy skies
  Upon morning summits laid;
Robe me in the purple and gold that flies
  Through thy shuttles of light and shade;
Let me rise and rejoice in thy smile aright,
  As mountains and forests do;
Let me welcome thy twilight and thy night,
  And wait for thy dawn anew!

Give me of the brook's faith, joyously sung
  Under clank of its icy chain!
Give me of the patience that hides among
  Thy hilltops in mist and rain!
Lift me up from the clod; let me breathe thy
    breath
  Thy beauty and strength give me!
Let me lose both the name and the meaning of
    death
  In the life that I share with thee!

—*Lucy Larcom.*

FAITH

I will not doubt, though all my ships at sea
　　Come drifting home with broken mast and sails;
　　I shall believe the Hand which never fails,
From seeming evil worketh good for me;
And though I weep because those sails are bat-
　　　　tered,
　　Still will I cry, while my best hopes lie shat-
　　　　tered,
　　　　　　　　　　　　"I trust in thee."

I will not doubt, though all my prayers return
　　Unanswered from the still, white Realm above;
　　I shall believe it is an all-wise Love
Which has refused those things for which I yearn;
And though at times I can not keep from grieving;
　　Yet the pure ardor of my fixed believing
　　　　　　　　Undimmed shall burn.

I will not doubt, though sorrows fall like rain,
　　And troubles swarm like bees about a hive;
　　I shall believe the heights for which I strive
Are only reached by anguish and by pain;
And though I groan and tremble with my crosses,
　　I yet shall see, through my severest losses,
　　　　　　　　The greater gain.

I will not doubt; well-anchored in the faith,
　　Like some staunch ship, my soul braves every
　　　　gale,
So strong its courage that it will not fail
To breast the mighty unknown sea of Death.
Oh, may I cry when body parts with spirit,
　　"I do not doubt," so listening worlds may hear it,
　　　　　　　　With my last breath.
　　　　　　　　　　—*Ella Wheeler Wilcox.*

IF LIFE WERE ALL

If life were all, and death its certain end,
  If nothing lured the soul to higher aims,
If what we cherish here and guard and tend,
  Were crown and summit of all life attains,
    Rewards so small, had scarce repaid the battle
      life sustains
If life were all.

Were there no faith that on another shore
  Beyond the distance of this life's utmost scope
Lay Beulah lands, where joy reigns ever more,
  Surpassing all things that hearts may hope
    Beneath life's pall it were not well, for these
      vain years to grope
If life were all.

If life were all, and amid its wild alarms
  No cross, no blood shone through its awful years,
If through its darkness no outstretched arms,
  Beckoned the woeful forsake his fears
    O, cup of gall; life were not worth its floodtide
      of tears
If life were all.   —*Anon.*

Young Woman

A SONG OF TRUST

I cannot always see the way that leads
  To heights above;
I sometimes quite forget he leads me on
  With hands of love;
But yet I know the path must lead me to
  Immanuel's land,
And when I reach life's summit, I shall know
  And understand.

I cannot always trace the onward course
    My ship must take;
  But, looking backward, I behold afar
    Its shining wake,
  Illumined with God's light of love; and so
    I onward go,
  In perfect trust that he who holds the helm
    The course must know.

I cannot always see the plan on which
    He builds my life;
For oft the sound of hammers, blow on blow,
    The noise of strife,
Confuse me till I quite forget he knows
    And oversees,
And that in all details with his good plan
    My life agrees.

I cannot always know and understand
    The Master's rule;
I cannot always do the tasks he gives
    In life's hard school;
But I am learning with his help to solve
    Them one by one;
And, when I cannot understand, to say,
    "Thy will be done!"

                —*Gertrude Curtis.*

               ⁂

SECRET OF SORROW

The summer rose the sun hath flushed
    With crimson glory, may be sweet
'Tis sweeter when its leaves are crushed
    Beneath the wind's and tempest's feet.

The rose that waves upon its tree
  In life sheds perfume all around
More sweet that perfume seems to me,
  Of roses trampled on the ground.

The living rose with every breath
  Scents carelessly the summer air
The wounded bleeds forth in death
  A richness far more sweet and rare.

It is a truth beyond our ken
  And yet a truth that all may read
As it is with roses so it is with men
  The sweetest hearts are hearts that bleed.

The Rose that Bethlehem saw bloom
  Out of a heart all full of grace
Gave never forth its full perfume
  Until the cross became its vase.
            —*Father Ryan.*

          ❧ ❧

GOD'S SURE HELP IN SORROW
    Leave all to God,
Forsaken one, and stay thy tears;
  For the Highest knows thy pain,
Sees thy suffering and thy fears;
  Thou shalt not wait his help in vain;
    Leave all to God.

    Be still and trust!
For his strokes are strokes of love,
  Thou must for thy profit bear;
He thy filial fear would move,
  Trust thy Father's loving care,
    Be still and trust!

Know God is near!
Though thou think'st him far away,
  Though his mercy long hath slept,
He will come and not delay,
  When his child enough hath wept,
    For God is near!

Oh, teach him not
When and how to hear thy prayers;
  Never doth our God forget;
He the cross who longest bears
  Finds his sorrow's bounds are set;
    Then teach him not!

If thou love him,
Walking truly in his ways,
  Then no trouble, cross or death
E'er shall silence faith and praise;
  All things serve thee here beneath,
    If thou love God!

—*Anon.*

❧ ❧

FAITH IN GOD

Thy will, O God, my lot ordains,
  Whate'er my lot in life may be;
My faith in thee its grasp retains,
  However harsh seems thy decree.
I know not what thy ways portend,
But this I know, thou art my Friend,
  And in my need thy help is near;
I know that thou canst ne'er deceive
The soul that will in thee believe—
  Then what have I from thee to fear?

My faith, O God, in thee is stayed,
  Tho' darkness veils thee from my sight;
No threatening ills make me afraid,
  For faith finds shelter in thy might,
In deepest gloom, when most forlorn,
I glimpse the reddening flush of morn,
  When lowering night shall flee away.
My faith for me a victory wins,
On earth my heavenly bliss begins—
  A foregleam of eternal day.

In strife sometimes my courage fails,
  But faith makes weakened valor strong;
When hell-born doubt my mind assails,
  Then chants my faith the victor's song.
More faith in God, more faith, I crave,
To vanquish fear, to make me brave,
  When raging tempests round me roar;
More faith, to wing my faltering feet,
To make my heavenward steps more fleet,
  Until I tread the shining shore.
                    —*W. S. McKenzie.*

Middle Aged Man or Woman

MY SAVIOUR'S HAND

That tender hand—in dark Gethsemane
  Raised in the prayer, "Thy will, not mine, be
      done!"—
Was torn and bleeding in the agony
  Through which my guilty soul salvation won.

That chastening hand sometimes doth sorely rest
  Upon me while the storms of sorrow fall,
Yet draws me till I lean upon his breast,
  And find in him my strength, my hope, my all.

That guiding hand leads me from day to day,
　And smooths my path across earth's desert drear;
It holds me fast—my sure and only stay—
　As life recedes, and heaven's lights appear.

Oh, loving hand, when shadows deepen fast,
　And in the gloom I hear death's billows foam,
Draw me so near my eyes rest at the last
　Upon the face of him who bears me home!
　　　　　　　　　　　—*Katherine Purvis.*

　　　　　　　&　&

Aged Man

THE PARTING HOUR

There's something in "the parting hour"
　Will chill the warmest heart—
Yet kindred, comrades, lovers, friends,
　Are fated all to part;
But this I've seen—and many a pang
　Has pressed it on my mind—
The one who goes is happier
　Than those he leaves behind.

No matter what the journey be—
　Adventurous, dangerous, far
To the wild deep, or black frontier,
　To solitude, or war—
Still something cheers the heart that dares,
　In all of human kind;
And they who go are happier
　Than those they leave behind.

The bride goes to the bridegroom's home
  With doubting and with tears,
But does not Hope her rainbow spread
  Across the cloudy fears?
Alas! the mother who remains,
  What comfort can she find
But this—the gone is happier
  Than the one she leaves behind.

Have you a trusty comrade dear—
  An old and valued friend?
Be sure your term of sweet concourse
  At length will have an end.
And when you part as part you will,
  Oh take it not unkind,
If he who goes is happier
  Than you he leaves behind.

God wills it so, and so it is;
  The pilgrims on their way,
Though weak and worn, more cheerful are
  Than all the rest who stay.
And when, at last, poor man, subdued,
  Lies down to death resigned,
May he not still be happier far
  Than those he leaves behind!

                              —*Edward Pollock.*

THE KINGLIEST KINGS

Ho, ye who in a noble work
  Win scorn, as flames draw air,
And in the way where lions lurk
  God's image bravely bear—
Tho' trouble-tired and torture-torn,
The kingliest kings are crowned with thorn.

Life's glory, like the bow in heaven,
  Still springeth from the cloud;
And Soul ne'er soared the starry Seven
  But Pain's fire-chariot rode.
They've battled best who've boldliest borne:
The kingliest kings are crowned with thorn.

The martyr's fire-crown on the brow
  Doth into glory burn;
And tears that from love's torn heart flow
  To pearls of spirit turn
Our dearest hopes in pangs are born,
The kingliest kings are crowned with thorn.

As beauty in death's cerement shrouds,
  And stars bejewel night,
God-splendors live in dim heart-clouds,
  And suffering worketh might.
The murkiest hour is mother o' morn,
The kingliest kings are crowned with thorn.
                              —*Gerald Massey.*

His form is famine-gaunt and bowed
  His aged hands have lost their skill;
But, like the moon within a cloud,
A hidden light his soul doth fill.

It shineth through his careworn face,
  And o'er his sordid garb it flings
The viewless mantle of a grace
  Not found in palaces of kings.

On journeys high his spirit fares,
  Of realms of sunless light is free;
The triumph of the saints he shares,
  He stands beside the Crystal Sea.

He hears the mystic anthem tone;
  He mingles with the tearless throng
Who meet before the Great White Throne;
  His voice uplifts the Wedding Song.
                                —*Anon.*

& &

Aged Woman
UNKNOWN HEROES

When God shall call the muster-roll,
  As heroes he'll mark off
Some who ne'er charged at Waterloo,
  Or stormed the Malakoff.

Stars, garters, crosses, ribbons, fade;
  New orders here unfold:
The widow's mite, St. Martin's cloak,
  The cup of water cold.

The hearts that saved the world by love
    And hourly Calvaries bore,
The mother-martyrs, queenly host,
    Are marshalled to the fore.

Earth's black-robed throngs are clad in white;
    Their brows a light adorns—
A radiance of diamond,
    Crowns of transfigured thorns.

Some humble folk we knew quite well,
    But passed with scarce a nod,
Now rank as heaven's nobility—
    The chivalry of God.

Imperial names of history
    Omitted from the list;
In Paradise, preferment shows
    A hidden satirist.

The heavens are taken by surprise;
    Archangels hold their breath;
Through audience multitudinous
    A stillness reigns like death.

Then flutterings of seraphs' wings—
    Applauding cherubim—
With joy long pent the skies are rent—
    A million eyes grow dim—

And down far-peopled spaces rolls
    A surge of gratitude,
That God from bitter grapes of life
    Should crush beatitude.

'Tis thus, with irony divine,
  Earth's judgments are reversed;
When God shall call the muster-roll
  The last will be the first.

                    —*George Alway.*

ℬ ℬ

THE BRAVEST BATTLE

The bravest battle that ever was fought
  Shall I tell you where and when?
On the maps of the world you will find it **not**,
  It was fought by the mothers of men.

Nay, not with cannon nor battle-shot
  With sword, or nobler pen;
Nay not with eloquent words of thought
  From mouths of wonderful men.

But deep in a walled-up woman's heart
  A woman who would not yield,
But bravely, silently bore her part—
  Lo! there was the battlefield!

No marshalling troops, no bivouac song—
  No banners to gleam and wave—
But, oh! these battles, they last so long—
  From babyhood to the grave.

Yet faithful still as a bridge of stars
  She fights in her walled-up town.
Fights on and on in her endles wars,
  Then, silent, unseen, goes down.

Oh, Ye, with banners and battle-shot
  With soldiers to shout and praise,
I tell you the kingliest victories wrought
  Are won in these silent ways.

Oh, spotless woman, in a world of shame
  With splendid and silent scorn,
Go back to God as pure as you came
  The queenliest warrior born.

—Joaquin Miller.

❧ ❧

A SILVERY LIGHT FOR EVERY CLOUD

For every cloud, a silvery light,
    God wills it so.
For every vale a shining height,
A glorious morn for every night,
    And birth for labor's throe.

For snow's white wing, a verdant field;
    A gain for loss,
For buried seed the harvest yield;
For pain a strength, a joy revealed,
    A crown for every cross.

❧ ❧

Heaven
THE UNBROKEN FAMILY

Love craves the presence and the sight of all its
  well-beloved.
And, therefore, weep we in the homes whence they
  are far removed;
Love craves the presence and the sight of each beloved one,
And, therefore, Jesus spoke the word which caught
  them to His throne. . . .

Thus heaven is gathering, one by one, in its capacious breast,
All that is pure and permanent, and beautiful and blest;

The family is scattered yet, though of one home and heart,
Part militant, in earthly gloom, in heavenly glory part.
But who can speak the rapture, when the circle is complete,
And all the children sundered now around one Father meet?
One fold, one Shepherd, one employ, one everlasting home:
"Lo! I come quickly." Even so. Amen! Lord Jesus, come!

—*E. H. Bickersteth.*

HOME OF THE CONQUERORS

Home of the conquerors! How bright,
  How glorious are thy walls of light!
Through Christ may we admittance win,
  And, late or early, enter in.

No clang of arms, no shouts, are there
  Borne on the ever tranquil air;
No hostile force is there descried,
  No murmurs heard of hate or pride.

O joy! when all our fears and ill
  Shall cease at Jesus' "Peace, be still!"
O joy, when, every conflict o'er,
  We shall be righteous evermore.

Who can conceive or who express
  The charms of perfect holiness?
The bliss of feeling beat within
  A heart made free from every sin?

Home of the conquerors! We press
  Towards thy seats of happiness;
Through Christ our Lord we fight, we win,
  And thy bright gates shall let us in!
                              —*E. A. W.*

     ❧ ❧

THE LAND BEYOND THE SEA

The Land beyond the Sea!
Sometimes distinct and near
It grows upon the eye and ear,
And the gulf narrows to a thread-like mere;
  We seem half way to thee,
  Calm Land beyond the Sea!

The Land beyond the Sea!
Oh, how the lapsing years,
'Mid our not unsubmissive tears,
Have borne, now singly, now in fleets, the biers
  Of those we love to thee,
  Calm Land beyond the Sea!

The Land beyond the Sea!
Why fadest thou in light?
Why art thou better seen towards night?
Dear Land! look always plain, look always bright,
  That we may gaze on thee,
  Calm Land beyond the Sea!
                    —*Frederick William Faber.*

REST

Rest—with each vision of the future blended
　Comes that bright hope, so soothing and so dear,
All the long journey past, the conflict ended,
　　Rest—but not here!

Not here! while war's alarm is ever sounding,
　While half the promised land is unpossessed,
On the red battle-plain, with foes surrounding,
　　Who dares to rest?

Not here! when autumn's sun is brightly shining,
　Yet storm-clouds gather in the darkening west,
On the ripe corn-fields, till the sun's declining,
　　Who thinks of rest?

Not here, but yonder—where in peace forever
　The faithful servants with their Lord are blest,
Where friends depart, and foes shall enter never—
　　There we shall rest.

Yes; and that prospect now the heart sustaineth
　Lightly each burden and each toil to bear;
For us the promise holds, the rest "remaineth,"
　　Not here—but there!

　　　　　　　　　　——*H. L. L.*

　　　　　⁂

NO MORE DEATH

No more death; no more sorrow, and no fears;
　No valley of the shadow, no more pain!
No weeping, for God dries away the tears,
　And dried by him tears never rise again.

No darkened room, no silence, and no cry
  Of bitterness as he recalls the breath;
No unfilled blank, no nameless agony;
  For he hath said, "There shall be no more
    death."

No more death! Then take comfort, ye who weep
  Give thanks to God, and raise the bowed head;
They are not lost—'tis "his beloved sleep,"
  And he who takes and keeps the holy dead.

Are they not safe with him? And when the veil
  Is rent for us, and sight supplanteth faith,
Then, reunited, love shall never fail;
  For he hath said, "There shall be no more
    death."

                                    —*H. Drummond.*

& &

HEAVEN AT LAST

Angel voices sweetly singing,
Echoes through the blue dome ringing,
News of wondrous gladness bringing;
  Ah, 'tis heaven at last!

On the jasper threshold standing,
Like a pilgrim safely landing;
See, the strange bright scene expanding,
  Ah, 'tis heaven at last!

Sin forever left behind us,
Earthly visions cease to blind us,
Earthly fetters cease to bind us;
  Ah, 'tis heaven at last!

Not a teardrop ever falleth,
Not a pleasure ever palleth,
Song to song forever calleth;
    Ah, 'tis heaven at last!

Christ himself the living splendor,
Christ the sunlight mild and tender;
Praises to the Lamb we render:
    Ah, 'tis heaven at last!

                  —*Doctor Bonar.*

CHRIST'S PROMISE

When I reach life's earthly bound,
And the shadows darken round,
All familiar things and dear
Fading fast from eye and ear—
In that hour of mortal smart,
Trembling flesh and failing heart,
Shall I find my anchor vain,
Parting in that latest strain?
Hear the Shepherd's voice of old,
Looking on his helpless fold,
Looking far, with gaze divine,
Down the ages' lengthening line—
'Every feeble sheep I know,
Life eternal I bestow,
None shall pluck them from my hand"—
Shall that word of promise stand?
Or, when countless foes affright,
Closing round in latest fight,
In that deadly hour and dim
Shall my soul be snatched from him?

"Heaven and earth shall pass away,
Not My words," so Christ doth say;
In death's grasp His Truth shall be
Shield and buckler unto thee.

—*H. A. B.*

❧ ❧

ONE BY ONE

Not sweeping up together, in whirlwind or in cloud,
In the hush of summer weather, or when storms are
        thundering loud
        But one by one we go
        In the sweetness none may know.

In secret love the Master to each one whispers low,
"I am at hand; work faster; behold, the sunset
        glow!"
        And each one smileth sweet
        Who hears the Master's feet.

Not pressing through the portals of the Celestial
        Town,
An army of flesh immortals, by the Lord of battles
        won;
        But one by one we come,
        To the Gate of the heavenly home.

That all the powers of heaven may shout aloud to
        God,
As each new robe of Life is given, bought by the
        Master's blood
        And the heavenly raptures dawn
        On the pilgrims, one by one

That to each the Voice of the Father may thrill in
  welcome sweet
And round each the angels gather, with songs, on
  the shining street,
    As one by one we go
    To the glory none may know.

               —*B. M.*

SAFE HOME

Safe home, safe home in port! Rent cordage, shat-
  tered deck,
Torn sails, provisions short, and only not a wreck:
    But oh! the joy upon the shore
    To tell our voyage-perils o'er!

The prize, the prize secure! the warrior nearly
  fell;
Bore all he could endure, and bore not always well;
    But he may smile at troubles gone
    Who sets the victor-garland on!

No more the foe can harm; no more of leaguered
  camp,
The cry of night-alarm, and need of ready lamp.
    And yet how nearly had he failed—
    How nearly had the foe prevailed!

The lamb is in the fold, in perfect safety penned;
The lion once had hold, and thought to make an
  end,
    But One came by with wounded side,
    And for the sheep the Shepherd died.

The exile is at home!—O nights and days of tears,
O longings not to roam, O sins and doubts and
    fears,
      What matter now? In heavenly day
      The King has wiped all tears away!
            —Hymn of the Greek Church.

JERUSALEM EXULTING

Jerusalem, exulting
  On that securest shore,
I hope thee, wish thee, sing thee,
  And love thee evermore!
I ask not for my merit;
  I seek not to deny
My merit is destruction,
  A child of wrath was I.
But yet with faith I venture
  And hope upon my way,
For those perennial guerdons
  I labor night and day; . . . .
And grace, sweet grace celestial
  Shall all its love display,
And David's Royal Fountain
  Purge every sin away.
O sweet and blessed country,
  Shall I ever see thy face?
O sweet and blessed country,
  Shall I ever win thy grace?
I have the hope within me
  To comfort and to bless;
Shall I ever win the prize itself?
  Oh, tell me, tell me, Yes!
Exult, O dust and ashes, the Lord shall be thy part;
His only, his forever, thou shalt be, and thou art!
          —Neale, from St. Bernard of Cluny.

HEAVEN

I sit and think, when the sunset's gold
  Is flushing river and hill and shore,
I shall one day stand by the water cold
  And list for the sound of the boatman's oar.
I shall watch for a gleam of the flapping sail,
  I shall hear the boat as it gains the strand,
I shall pass from sight with the boatman pale,
  To the better shore of the spirit land.
I shall know the loved who have gone before,
  And joyfully sweet will the meeting be,
When over the river, the peaceful river,
  The angel of death shall carry me.
               —*N. A. W. Priest.*

❧ ❧

NO NIGHT IN HEAVEN

No night shall be in Heaven; no gathering gloom
Shall o'er that glorious landscape ever come.
No tears shall fall in sadness o'er those flowers,
That breathe their fragrance through celestial
  bowers.

No night shall be in Heaven, no dreadful hour
Of mental darkness, or the tempter's power.
Across those skies no envious clouds shall roll,
To dim the sunlight of the raptured soul.

No night shall be in Heaven; no sorrow's reign,
No secret anguish, no corporeal pain;
No shivering limbs, no burning fever there;
No soul's eclipse, no winter of despair.

No night shall be in Heaven, but endless noon;
No fast declining sun, no waning moon;
But there the Lamp shall yield perpetual light,
'Mid pastures green, and waters ever bright.

—Anon.

   ❦ ❦

THE BEAUTIFUL LAND

Full oft do I dream of the Beautiful Land
  That lies over the mystical river—
And my soul seems to follow the beckoning hand
That guides me along till my forehead seems fanned
  By the breeze which is fragrant forever.

And the sorrows of earth, like a hideous dream,
  Dissolve in the sunlight of heaven—
And I wander by many a radiant stream,
Whose musical waters flash back in the gleam
  Of a day that fades not into even—

And magical blooms that are wondrously fair,
  Lie spread out like visions before me—
And a spell of enchantment is borne on the air
That steals from the heart every shadow of care,
  And sheds sweet tranquility o'er me.

There Mercy and Love wander, hand clasped in
    hand,
  And Faith twines her wreath of 'Mortelles—
And the sky—by God's rainbow of tenderness
    spanned—
Reflects on its bosom the Beautiful Land—
  Its angels and glittering portals.

—D. W. Gwin.

Weddings

Notes On Ministerial Conduct at Weddings

1. The wedding ceremony should be neither too long nor yet too short. Many couples will ask for a short ceremony. On the other hand, frequently the minister is called upon to perform marriage ceremonies at formal home weddings or church weddings; in these, a longer and more stately ceremony is desired. Hence, every pastor or minister should have at least two marriage ceremonies, one brief and one longer and more stately in its makeup.

2. The marriage ceremony is among the most solemn of the ceremonies of life. The minister will do well to remember this. Many of them will be tempted to make use of poetic, florid, and high-sounding sentences in their ceremonies. They should be careful to avoid an extreme in this respect. They should remember that things can be both beautiful and stately, and that in seeking to string together a lot of beautiful words, composing beautiful sentences, stateliness and dignity can be sacri-

ficed to the practical ruin of the impressiveness of the ceremony.

3. Most ministers prepare their own ceremonies, but the same line of thought runs through them all, the only material difference consisting in the terms and expressions used. Many ministers memorize their ceremonies and use them without the aid of a book. It is the opinion of this writer that fewer mistakes are made and a more general impressiveness is added to the whole occasion where the ceremony is read from some book or from the typewritten page.

4. The demand today for the ring ceremony is almost universal, and very often the modern minister is requested to use the double ring ceremony. Every minister should prepare himself for using the ring ceremonies so that he may perform them with grace. The model ceremonies given in this book were prepared by men who have had long experience in pastoral work and who have been very popular with couples desiring to be married.

5. The minister should be very careful of his dress at weddings, especially if they are formal affairs, either in the church or in the home. He is not required to wear approved evening dress clothes at full dress weddings, but he should wear the approved full dress

for the pulpit. Twenty years ago this consisted in a Prince Albert suit, as it was commonly called. Now a neat cut-away is all that is necessary, but the pastor or minister should by no means wear a sack suit or other informal or business clothes at a formal wedding. He is at perfect liberty to do so, however, in the case of weddings where the parties on short notice go either to his home or to his study for the ceremony. On all other occasions it is better for the pastor to wear formal pulpit dress. Where a minister is in doubt about his attire, he should consult a first class clothier, who can always give correct information.

6. Very often the pastor is consulted in making arrangements for the church wedding and is asked to take part in the rehearsal. In many cases he will be asked to suggest to the young people just how the whole thing may be carried out properly. Therefore, it is well for the young minister to familiarize himself with the very best customs in order that he may be thoroughly prepared to advise his young people when necessity requires.

7. A formal church wedding is usually, though not always, celebrated in the evening. Sometimes it is celebrated at another hour of

the day such as high noon. But the standard custom favors the evening hour. It is a full-dress affair. Fashions in full-dress change as do other fashions. Usually the young people are familiar with the fashions of the time. On such occasions the following parties are necessary to the proper observance of the affair: two or more bridesmaids, two or more ushers or groomsmen, the maid or matron of honor, the best man, the ring-bearer, the flower girl, in addition to the bride and groom. Sometimes also the father or other male relative of the bride may be included to give the bride away. Usually there are musicians who sing appropriate selections immediately preceding the ceremony, or else give instrumental numbers. The ushers or groomsmen are present when the doors are opened and are charged with the responsibility of seating the people in proper order. After the special music has been rendered the organist begins the wedding march. Then the following procedure is observed. The minister enters the church from a side door or steps from some obscure corner and proceeds with deliberate step to the altar. At the same time one of the groomsmen and one of the bridesmaids start from the heads of the aisles of the church and proceed to the altar with measured step, the groomsman going down the aisle to the right of the minister and the bridesmaid going down the opposite aisle. Upon their arrival at the altar they meet and pass each other, taking their stands, the groomsman to the extreme left of the minister and the bridesmaid to his extreme right. These are followed by the other groomsmen and bridesmaids in proper order, who also meet and pass each other at the altar and take their stand, the groomsmen to the left and the bridesmaids to the right of the minister. Then follow the ring-bearer, going down the left aisle, and the flower girl, going down the right aisle. Upon their arrival at the altar the ring-bearer stands on the immediate left of the minister and the flower girl on his right. Then the bride with her maid or matron of honor proceeds down the right aisle, while the groom with his best man proceeds down the left aisle. When they meet at the altar the maid or matron of honor releases the bride who takes the arm of the groom as they two stand immediately in front of the minister. The maid or matron of honor remains at the side of the bride but a step away, while the best man stands at the side of the groom but a step away. If the father gives the bride away, then the maid or matron of honor precedes the bride and her father down the aisle and stands a little to one side until the father has escorted the bride to the side of the groom. Then the maid or matron of honor stands at the side of the bride but a step away. The father after escorting the bride to the groom either joins his family in the second pew or steps back to one side of the altar. When the ceremony is completed the ringbearer and flower girl lead the procession out the right aisle. As they go the flower girl scatters flowers. They are followed by the bride and groom, who in turn are followed by the maid of honor and best man, and these in turn are followed by the several couples of bridesmaids and groomsmen. This order is varied to suit the whims of the contracting parties or to conform to the different architectural types in church buildings. But this is the standard custom. In most instances there are always present those who are familiar with the best customs and who can give the necessary information. These instructions are included for the benefit of young ministers who wish to familiarize themselves with the best customs before they have actual opportunity to observe or practice them.

8. Marriage is both a civil and a divine contract. Consequently it is not lawful with-

out a license issued by the authorized authorities. A minister cannot perform the marriage ceremony unless the license is in his possession. Therefore, he should take care to see that somebody, the groom or best man, turns the license over to him before the time set for the wedding. This custom will obviate embarrassment very often. The minister should remember that the contracting parties are usually excited and are therefore liable to overlook even so important a matter. Then it may be that they are not informed and do not really know that the license must be in the hands of the minister. Let the minister himself look after this detail.

9. Year by year the legal requirements of marriage become more strict. These requirements differ in the several states. The minister should seek to know the requirements immediately after he takes up his residence in a new state in order that he may fulfil them and be ready to perform the marriage ceremony according to the law of that state. In one state the minister must give bond, in another he must have his credentials recorded in the circuit clerk's office, and in another state he must give his title and position as his authority for performing the marriage ceremony. Because of these varying requirements min-

isters have found themselves embarrassed. This can be avoided by inquiry at the court house as soon as the minister enters upon a new work in a new state.

Marriage Ceremony

By James Randolph Hobbs, D.D., LL.D.

Holy and happy is the sacred hour when two devoted hearts are bound by the enchanting ties of matrimony. And these precious evidences of purity of heart and contentment of mind, for all their future, are made more sure, when the contracting parties enter this glad time, clad in the comely robes of reverence, humility, and faith, that they may then be blessed of our Heavenly Father, Maker of us all—the One who has ordained marriage as the cornerstone of family life and the guarantee of honorable human society.

First and noblest of human contracts, marriage was divinely instituted when Jehovah God spoke the nuptial words to Adam and Eve in the Garden of Eden. Jesus of Nazareth honored its celebration by his presence at the wedding in Cana of Galilee, and chose its beautiful relations as the figure of that benign union between himself and his Church. Paul, militant missionary Apostle, commends it as a worthy institution, alike essential to social order, human efficiency, and well-being while the race inhabits the earth, and tells the husband to love his wife as Christ loved his Church and gave himself for it, and the wife to be faithful to her husband, even as the Church is obedient to Christ in everything. Thus the two, husband and wife, forsaking all others become one flesh, one in thought, intent, and hope, in all the concerns of the present life.

You——————, and You——————, having come to me signifying your desire to be formally united in marriage, and being assured that no legal, moral, or religious barriers hinder this proper union, I command you to join your right hands and give heed to the questions now asked you.

——————In taking the woman whom you hold by the right hand to be your lawful and wedded wife, I require you to promise to love and cherish her, to honor and sustain her, in sickness as in health, in poverty as in wealth, in the bad that may darken your days, in the good that may light your ways, and to be true to her in all things until death alone shall part you.

Do you so promise?

——————In taking the man who holds you by the right hand to be your lawful and wedded husband, I require you to promise to love and cherish him, to honor and sustain him, in sickness as in health, in poverty as in wealth, in the bad that may darken your days, in the good that may light your ways, and to be true to him in all things until death alone shall part you.

Do you so promise?

Then are you devoted to each other until death parts you.

(If the ring ceremony is desired, the minister will take the ring from the receptacle of the ring-bearer, or from the groomsman, and read the following):

From time immemorial, the ring has been used to seal important covenants. When the race was young and parliaments unknown, the great seal of State was fixed upon a ring worn by the reigning monarch, and its stamp was the sole sign of imperial authority. Friends often exchanged the simple band of gold as enduring evidence of good will, while many a hero and heroine of immortal song and thrilling tale threaded winding paths of intrigue and adventure, safe and unhurt, bearing as a magic talisman the signet of some great benefactor. From such impressive precedents the golden circlet, most prized of jewels, has come to its loftiest prestige in the symbolic significance it vouches at the hymeneal altar. Here untarnishable material and unique form become the precious tokens of the pure and abiding qualities of the ideal marital state.

(The minister hands the ring to the groom, instructing him to place it upon the third finger of the bride's left hand and to hold it while the minister propounds the following questions):

Do you———— give this ring to————as a token of your love for her?

The man shall answer, I do.

Will you———— take this ring as a token of ————'s love for you and will you wear it as a token of your love for him?

The woman shall answer, I will.

(Where the double ring ceremony is desired, the minister will take the other ring from the receptacle of the ring-bearer, or from the groomsman and hand it to the bride, instructing her to place it upon the third finger of the groom's left hand and to hold it in place while the minister propounds the following questions):

Do you———— give this ring to———— as a token of your love for him?

The woman shall answer, I do.

Will you———— take this ring as a token of————'s love for you, and will you wear it as a token of your love for her?

The man shall answer, I will.

(The minister will now instruct the couple to rejoin their right hands, after which he will repeat the following):

Having pledged your faith in, and love to, each other, and having sealed your solemn marital vows by giving and receiving the ring (or rings), acting in the authority vested in me by the laws of this State, and looking to Heaven for divine sanction, I pronounce you husband and wife in the presence of God and these assembled witnesses. Therefore, let all men take care in the sight of God this holy covenant shall ever remain sacred.

Prayer:

Holy, Righteous, and Merciful Father, alike Creator, Preserver, and Redeemer of mankind, fill these thy servants with a deep sense of the solemn obligations which they have just assumed. Guide them to look to thee for grace in their efforts to discharge these obligations with honor to themselves, in thy sight and in the sight of men. Ordain that their love now mutually plighted, may never falter whatever course life may take with them. Crown their lives with loving-kindness and tender mercies, and provide for their protection while they travel the uneven way that leads from now to the end. Give them a rich measure of material prosperity, and lead them into the fulness of spiritual understanding and holy living, that they may have an abundant entrance into the joys everlasting. So we pray through Jesus Christ our Lord.

The Lord bless and keep you. The Lord make his face to shine upon you and be gracious unto you. The Lord lift up his countenance upon you and give you peace, through Jesus Christ our Lord. Amen.

Marriage Ceremony
(From the Alabama Book of Legal Forms)

Marriage is an institution of divine appointment and is commended as honorable among all men. It is the most important step in life and should not therefore be entered into unadvisedly or lightly, but discreetly and soberly.

In this estate these two persons come now to be joined. If any person present can show cause why they may not lawfully be joined together, let him now speak or else hereafter forever hold his peace.

(Addressing the couple the one performing ceremony continues):

I solemnly require and charge you both, as you hope for joy and peace in the marriage state, if either of you know any just cause why you may not be lawfully joined together in matrimony, you do now confess it.

It is then your will to proceed?

(The parties must now join right hands):

To the man: Do you, sir, take this woman to be your lawful wife and do you promise before God and these witnesses, to love her, comfort her, honor and keep her in sickness and in health, and forsaking all others keep thee only unto her so long as you both shall live?

The man shall answer, I do.

To the woman: Do you take this man to be your lawful husband; and do you solemnly promise before God and these witnesses that you will love, honor, and keep him in sickness and in health, and forsaking all others keep thee only unto him so long as you both shall live?

The woman shall answer, I do.

(If the parties wish to use the ring, the minister shall instruct the man to place the ring on the third finger of the woman's left hand and hold as he repeats after the minister):

"With this ring I thee wed and with all my worldly goods I thee endow, in the name of the Father and of the Son and of the Holy Ghost. Amen." (Or according to the creed of the parties contracting).

Inasmuch as this man and this woman have in the presence of God and these witnesses consented together to be joined in the lawful bonds of matrimony and thereto have given and pledged their troth each to the other (and if a ring is used: have declared the same by giving and receiving a ring), I now according to the ordinances of God and in the name of the State of Alabama, pronounce them husband and wife. "What therefore God hath joined together let not man put asunder."

And now may the God of peace prosper and bless you in this new relation, and may the grace of Jesus Christ abound unto you now and always.   Amen.

Marriage Ceremony By J. J. Taylor. D.D., LL.D.

We desire, our Father, to acknowledge thee in all our ways, that thou mayest direct our steps. Especially do we need thee in the epochs of life. Graciously regard thy servants who come before thee to assume the mutual obligations involved in marriage. May they walk not heedlessly, but in thy fear, in the solemn step which they are about to take. Assure them and us of thy presence; and let the beauty of the Lord our God be upon us in the rite we celebrate. We humbly ask it for Jesus' sake. Amen.

Address:

Marriage is God's first institution for the welfare of the race. In the quiet bowers of Eden before the forbidden tree had yielded its fateful fruit or the tempter had touched the world, God saw that it was not good for the man to be alone. He made an help suitable for him, and established the rite of marriage, while heavenly hosts witnessed the wonderful scene.

Originated in divine wisdom and goodness, designed to promote human happiness and holiness, this rite is the foundation of home life and social order, and must so remain till the end of time. It was sanctioned and honored by the presence and power of Jesus at the marriage in Cana, of Galilee, and marked the beginning of his wondrous works. It is declared by the apostle to be honorable in all. So it is ordained that a man shall leave his father and mother, and cleave unto his wife; and they twain shall be one flesh, united in hopes and aims and sentiments in all the interests of this present time.

The Test:

If ye, then, —————— and —————— have freely and deliberately chosen each other as partners in this holy estate, and know of no just cause why ye should not be so united, in token thereof ye will please join your right hands.

Groom's Vow:

——————, in taking the woman you hold by the right hand to be your lawful and wedded wife, before God and the witnesses present you must promise to love her, to honor and cherish her in that relation, and leaving all others cleave only unto her, and be to her in all things a true and faithful husband so long as you both shall live. Do you so promise?

Answer:

I do.

Bride's Vow:

————, in taking the man you hold by the right hand to be your lawful and wedded husband, before God and the witnesses present you must promise to love him, to honor and cherish him in that relation, and leaving all others, cleave only unto him, and to be to him in all things a true and faithful wife so long as you both shall live. Do you so promise?

Answer:

I do.

Minister's Response:

Then are ye each given to the other for richer or poorer, for better or worse, in sickness and in health, till death shall part you.

The Token:

And as a ceaseless reminder of this hour and of the vows you have taken, place this ring on the hand of your bride and repeat after me: "With this ring I thee wed, with loyal love I thee endow, and all my worldly goods with thee I share, in the name of the Father and the Son and the Holy Ghost, blessed forever more. Amen."

Prayer (in words like these):

We thank thee, O God, for the providence which brings human hearts into the bonds of human love, so like the love divine. Accept in heaven, thy dwelling place, the union of hearts which has here been confessed before thee, and let thy blessing rest thereon.

Grant that the ties which bind these thy servants may grow stronger with the passing years. May they trust each other with perfect confidence, and together trust in thee for guidance and help in all the way that lies before them. Prosper them in temporal things according to thy purposes in grace. Especially do thou admit them to the bounty of thy spiritual favors; and in the end may they triumph through faith and find an abundant entrance into thine everlasting kingdom. And to Father, Son, and Holy Ghost shall be praises ever more. Amen.

Declaration:

For as much, then, as ——— and ———
have covenanted together according to the
teachings of the Scriptures and laws of the
state, I as an officer of the law and a minister
of the gospel declare that they are husband
and wife. "What therefore God hath joined
together, let not man put asunder."

Benediction:

The grace of the Lord Jesus Christ, the love
of God, the fellowship of the Holy Ghost,
abide with you for ever more. Amen.

The Episcopal Marriage Service

(At the day and time appointed for the solemnization of matrimony, the persons to be married shall come into the body of the church, or shall be ready in some proper house, with their friends and neighbors: and there standing together, the man on the right hand, and the woman on the left, the minister shall say):

Dearly beloved: We are gathered together here in the sight of God, and in the face of this company, to join together this man and this woman in holy matrimony; which is commended of St. Paul to be honorable among all men; and therefore is not by any to be entered into unadvisedly or lightly; but reverently, discreetly, advisedly, and in the fear of God. Into this holy estate, these two persons come now to be joined. If any man can show just cause why they may not lawfully be joined together, let him now speak, or else hereafter forever hold his peace.

And, also, speaking unto the persons who are to be married he shall say:

I require and charge you both, as ye will answer in the dreadful Day of Judgment, when the secrets of all hearts shall be disclosed, that if either of you knows any impediment why ye may not be lawfully joined together in matrimony, ye do now confess it. For be ye well assured, that if any persons are joined together otherwise than as God's Word doth allow, their marriage is not lawful.

If no impediment shall be alleged, the minister shall say to the man:

M., Wilt thou have this woman to be thy wedded wife, to live together after God's ordinance, in the holy estate of matrimony? Wilt thou love her, comfort her, honor and keep her, in sickness and in health; and, forsaking all others, keep thee only unto her, so long as ye both shall live?

The man shall answer, I will. Then shall the minister say to the woman:

N., Wilt thou have this man to be thy wedded husband, to live together after God's ordinance, in the holy estate of matrimony? Wilt thou obey him and serve him, love, honor, and keep him in sickness and in health; and forsaking all others, keep thee only unto him, so long as ye both shall live?

The woman shall answer, I will. Then shall the minister say:

Who giveth this woman to be married to this man?

Then shall they give their troth to each other in
this manner: The minister, receiving the woman at
her father's or friend's hand, shall cause the man
with his right hand to take the woman by her right
hand, and to say after him as follows:

I, M., take thee, N., to my wedded wife,
to have and to hold from this day forward, for
better for worse, for richer for poorer, in
sickness and in health, to love and to cherish,
till death do us part according to God's holy
ordinance; and thereto I plight thee my troth.

Then shall they loose their hands; and the
woman with her right hand taking the man by his
right hand, shall likewise say after the minister:

I, N., take thee, M., to my wedded husband,
to have and to hold from this day forward,
for better for worse, for richer for poorer,
in sickness and in health, to love, to cherish
and to obey, till death do us part, according
to God's holy ordinance; and thereto I give
thee my troth.

Then shall they again loose their hands; and the
man shall give unto the woman a ring. And the minister taking the ring shall deliver it unto the man,
to put it upon the third finger of the woman's left
hand. And the man, holding the ring there, and
taught by the minister, shall say:

With this ring I thee wed, and with all my
worldly goods I thee endow: in the name of
the Father, and of the Son and of the Holy
Ghost. Amen.

Then the man leaving the ring upon the woman's left hand, the minister shall say:

Let us pray:

Our Father, who art in Heaven, hallowed be thy name; Thy kingdom come; Thy will be done on earth, as it is in Heaven; Give us this day our daily bread: And forgive us our trespasses, as we forgive them that trespass against us; And lead us not into temptation; But deliver us from evil. Amen.

O eternal God, creator and preserver of all mankind, giver of all spiritual grace, the author of everlasting life; send thy blessing upon these thy servants, this man and this woman, whom we bless in thy name; that, as Isaac and Rebecca lived faithfully together, so these persons may surely perform and keep the vow and covenant betwixt them made, whereof this ring given and received is a token and pledge, and may ever remain in perfect love and peace together, and live according to thy laws; through Jesus Christ our Lord. Amen.

Then shall the minister join their right hands together and say:

"What therefore God hath joined together, let not man put asunder."

Then shall the minister speak unto the company:

Forasmuch as M., and N., have consented together in holy wedlock, and have witnessed the same before God and this company, and hereto have given and pledged their troth, each to the other, and have declared the same by giving and receiving a ring, and by joining hands; I pronounce that they are man and wife, in the name of the Father, and of the Son, and of the Holy Ghost. Amen.

And the minister shall add this blessing, the candidates kneeling, and the minister putting his hands upon their heads:

God the Father, God the Son, God the Holy Ghost, bless, preserve, and keep you: The Lord mercifully with his favor look upon you, and fill you with all spiritual benediction and grace; that ye may so live together in this life, that in the world to come ye may have life everlasting. Amen.

The Church

How to Organize a Church

A Baptist church is a body of people who have believed on Jesus Christ unto their salvation, have been baptized into the fellowship of his death and resurrection and have been organized on the plan and for the purposes of a Christian church as outlined by Jesus Christ and his apostles in the New Testament.

When it seems necessary to organize a Baptist church in any locality care should be exercised by those interested to establish whether or not there is a real need for such a church and a hopeful future of enlarging usefulness before it. To this end those interested should meet together several times and discuss the matter fully, making it an object of serious and earnest prayer. Also they should advise with leading pastors and brethren of other neighboring churches.

When it has been decided to organize a church, the organization may be effected in any one of three ways.

First: Those interested may meet together, choose a temporary moderator and clerk from their own number, formulate a resolution like the one that follows later in this chapter, adopt the same by a rising vote and by signature of the document, and proceed to the election of officers and the discharge of such other business and functions as are proper to a Baptist church.

Second: Those interested may invite one or more pastors or ordained ministers to be present at a meeting as suggested above for the purpose of giving counsel. When the meeting has come to order a temporary moderator and clerk may be chosen. If the visiting ministers approve the action, those interested may proceed to organization as outlined above.

Third: The safest and most approved procedure is that those who are interested in the organization of a church hold a mass meeting, at which time they adopt a resolution, inviting three or more neighboring churches to send representatives for the purpose of forming a council, under whose direction the church will be organized. When the people in the council have come together, the council should organize by choosing a moderator and clerk. After devotional exercises the council is then ready to hear reasons advanced by those interested for the organization of a church in that particular locality. After the matter is fully discussed, if the council is then of the opinion that such a church should be organized, they will proceed in the following order: a resolution, worded something like the following, should be prepared in advance and ready to submit for approval:

"Whereas, it appears to us that there is a real need for a Baptist church in this locality and after much prayer and seeking of divine guidance, and much consultation with our neighboring brethren and churches, and after the calling of a council to consider the matter, which council has voted that there is a need for such a church, it is resolved that we* ———— ———— ———— ———— do now enter upon the organization of a church under the direction of the council, composed of the following members ———— ———— ———— ———— representing the following churches, ———— ———— ———— ———— by the adoption of our church covenant, which is as follows:

*All those entering the organization of the church should present letters of dismission from other churches of like faith and order. As each name is proposed as a charter member of the new church the clerk should read the letter of dismission of the individual whose name is called.

CHURCH COVENANT

"Having been led, as we believe, by the Spirit of God, to receive the Lord Jesus Christ as our Saviour, and on the profession of our faith, having been baptized in the name of the Father, and of the Son, and of the Holy Ghost, we do now in the presence of God, angels, and this assembly, most solemnly and joyfully enter into covenant with one another, as one body in Christ.

"We engage therefore, by the aid of the Holy Spirit, to walk together in Christian love; to strive for the advancement of this church in knowledge, holiness, and comfort; to promote its prosperity and spirituality, to sustain its worship, ordinances, discipline, and doctrines; to contribute cheerfully and regularly to the support of the ministry, the expenses of the church, the relief of the poor, and the spread of the gospel through all nations.

"We also engage to maintain family and secret devotion; to religiously educate our children; to seek the salvation of our kindred and acquaintances; to walk circumspectly in the world; to be just in our dealings, faithful in our engagements, and exemplary in our deportment; to avoid all tattling, backbiting, and excessive anger. To abstain from the sale and use of intoxicating drinks as a beverage, and to be zealous in our efforts to advance the kingdom of our Saviour.

"We further engage to watch over one another in brotherly love; to remember each other in prayer, to aid each other in sickness and distress; to cultivate Christian sympathy in feeling and courtesy in speech; to be slow to take offense, but always ready for reconciliation, and mindful of the rules of our Saviour to secure it without delay.

"We moreover engage that when we remove from this place, we will as soon as possible unite with some other church, where we can carry out the spirit of this covenant and the principles of God's Word."

By the adoption of the following articles of faith:

Declaration of Faith

I. Of the Scriptures

"We believe that the Holy Bible was written by men divinely inspired, and is a perfect treasure of heavenly instruction; that it has God for its author, salvation for its end, and truth without any mixture of error for its matter; that it reveals the principles by which God will judge us; and therefore is, and shall remain to the end of the world, the true center of Christian union, and the supreme standard by which all human conduct, creeds and opinions shall be tried.

II. Of the True God

"We believe that there is one, and only one living and true God, an infinite, intelligent Spirit, whose name is JEHOVAH, the Maker and Supreme Ruler of heaven and earth; inexpressibly glorious in holiness, and worthy of all possible honor, confidence, and love; that in the unity of the Godhead there are three persons, the Father, the Son, and the Holy Ghost; equal in every divine perfection, and executing distinct but harmonious offices in the great work of redemption.

III. Of the Fall of Man

"We believe that man was created in holiness, under the law of his Maker; but by voluntary transgression fell from the holy and happy state; in consequence of which all mankind are now sinners, not by constraint but choice; being by nature utterly void of that holiness required by the law of God, positively inclined to evil; and therefore under just condemnation to eternal ruin, without defence or excuse.

IV. Of the Way of Salvation

"We believe that the salvation of sinners is wholly of grace; through the mediatorial offices of the Son of God; who by the appointment of the Father, freely took upon him our nature, yet without sin; honored the divine law by his personal obedience, and by his death made a full atonement for our sins; that having risen from the dead, he is now enthroned in heaven; and uniting in his wonderful person the tenderest sympathies with divine perfections, he is in every way qualified to be a suitable, a compassionate, and an all-sufficient Saviour.

V. Of Justification

"We believe that the great gospel blessing which Christ secures to such as believe in him is justification; that justification included the pardon of sin, and the promise of eternal life on principles of righteousness; that it is bestowed, not in consideration of any works of righteousness which we have done, but solely through faith in the Redeemer's blood; by virtue of which faith his perfect righteousness is freely imputed to us of God; that it brings us into a state of most blessed peace and favor with God, and secures every other blessing needful for time and eternity.

VI. Of the Freeness of Salvation

"We believe that the blessings of salvation are made free to all by the gospel; that it is the immediate duty of all to accept them by a cordial, penitent, and obedient faith; and that nothing prevents the salvation of the greatest sinner on earth, but his own inherent depravity and voluntary rejection of the gospel; which rejection involves him in an aggravated condemnation.

VII. Of Grace in Regeneration

"We believe that in order to be saved, sinners must be regenerated, or born again; that regeneration consists in giving a holy disposition to the mind; that it is effected in a manner above our comprehension by the power of the Holy Spirit, in connection with divine truth, so as to secure our voluntary obedience to the gospel; and that its proper evidence appears in the holy fruits of repentance, and faith, and newness of life.

VIII. Of Repentance and Faith

"We believe that repentance and faith are sacred duties, and also inseparable graces, wrought in our souls by the regenerating Spirit of God; whereby being deeply convinced of our guilt, danger, and helplessness, and of the way of salvation by Christ, we turn to God with unfeigned contrition, confession, and supplication for mercy; at the same time heartily receiving the Lord Jesus Christ as our Prophet, Priest, and King, and relying upon him alone as the only and all-sufficient Saviour.

IX. Of God's Purpose of Grace

"We believe that election is the eternal purpose of God, according to which he graciously regenerates, sanctifies, and saves sinners; that being perfectly consistent with the free agency of man, it comprehends all the means in connection with the end; that it is a most glorious display of God's sovereign goodness, being infinitely free, wise, holy, and unchangeable; that it utterly excludes boasting, and promotes humility, love, prayer, praise, trust in God, and active imitation of his free mercy; that it encourages the use of means in the highest degree; that it may be ascertained by its effect in all who truly believe the gospel; that it is the foundation of Christian assurance; and to ascertain it with regard to ourselves demands and deserves the utmost diligence.

X. Of Sanctification

"We believe that sanctification is the process by which, according to the will of God, we are made partakers of his holiness; that it is a progressive work; that it is begun in regeneration; and that it is carried on in the hearts of believers by the presence and power of the Holy Spirit, the Sealer, and Comforter, in the continual use of the appointed means— especially, the Word of God, self-examination, self-denial, watchfulness, and prayer.

XI. Of the Perseverance of Saints

"We believe that such only are real believers as endure unto the end; that their persevering attachment to Christ is the grand mark which distinguishes them from superficial professors; that a special providence watches over their welfare, and that they are kept by the power of God through faith unto salvation.

XII. Of the Harmony of the Law and the Gospel

"We believe that the law of God is the eternal and unchangeable rule of moral government; that it is holy, just, and good; and that the inability which the Scriptures ascribe to fallen men to fulfil its precepts, arises entirely from their love of sin: to deliver them from which, and to restore them through a Mediator to unfeigned obedience to the holy law, is one great end of the gospel, and of the means of grace connected with the establish· ment of the visible church.

XIII. Of a Gospel Church

"We believe that a visible church of Christ is a congregation of baptized believers, associated by covenant in the faith and fellowship of the gospel; observing the ordinances of Christ; governed by his laws; and exercising the gifts, rights, and privileges invested in them by his word; that its only Scriptural officers are bishops or pastors and deacons, whose qualifications, claims, and duties are defined in the Epistles of Timothy and Titus.

XIV. Of Baptism and the Lord's Supper

"We believe that Christian baptism is the immersion in water of a believer, into the name of the Father, and Son, and Holy Ghost: to show forth in a solemn and beautiful emblem, our faith in the crucified, buried, and risen Saviour, with its effect, in our death to sin and resurrection to a new life; that it is prerequisite to the privileges of a church relation; and to the Lord's Supper, in which the members of the church by the sacred use of bread and wine, are to commemorate together the dying love of Christ; preceded always by solemn self-examination.

XV. Of the Christian Sabbath

"We believe that the first day of the week is the Lord's Day, or Christian Sabbath; and is to be kept sacred to religious purposes, by abstaining from all secular labor and sinful recreation, by the devout observance of all the means of grace both private and public; and by preparation for that rest that remaineth for the people of God.

XVI. Of Civil Government

"We believe that civil government is of divine appointment, for the interests and good order of human society; and that magistrates are to be prayed for, conscientiously honored, and obeyed, except only in things opposed to the will of our Lord Jesus Christ, who is the only Lord of the conscience and the Prince of the kings of the earth.

XVII. Of the Righteous and the Wicked

"We believe that there is a radical and essential difference between the righteous and the wicked; that such only as through faith are justified in the name of the Lord Jesus, and sanctified by the Spirit of our God, are truly righteous in his esteem; while all such as continue in impenitence and unbelief are in his sight wicked, and under the curse; and this distinction holds among men, both in and after death.

XVIII. Of the World to Come

"We believe that the end of this world is approaching; that in the last day Christ will descend from heaven, and raise the dead from the grave to final retribution; that a solemn separation will then take place; that the wicked will be adjudged to endless punishment, and the righteous to endless joy; and that this Judgment will fix forever the final state of men in heaven or hell, on principles of righteousness."

By the choice of the following name:

"——— ——— Baptist Church"; and by the choice of such officers as may now seem advisable.

Resolved, second, that these resolutions be signed by all parties hereto and be spread in full upon the minute book of the church.

This resolution should be adopted by a rising vote and formally signed by all the parties immediately thereafter.

Then the council may give the right hand of fellowship to the members of the new church, assist them by the choice of the usual officers (moderator, temporary or permanent, a clerk and treasurer, and one deacon at least should be chosen). The church is then ready to perform any of the functions that properly belong to a Baptist church.

This plan of procedure may be altered somewhat in detail, as the circumstances may seem to require, but in general some such procedure as that outlined above is essential to the proper organization of the church.

Every Baptist church will want to be connected with the organized work of the denomination. Therefore, when it comes to ask for membership in its district association, if it has been regularly organized, no question will be raised; if on the other hand there has been irregularity in its organization, embarrassing questions may be raised. That is why we urge regular procedure in such matters.

Order of Service for Organizing a Baptist Church

1. Devotional services. (Songs, Scripture reading, and prayer).

2. Choice of temporary moderator and clerk. (If the first method is used as outlined above, all interested have part in choosing these officers. If the second method is used these officers are chosen from the ministers present, and if the third method is used the council chooses its own officers).

3. Statement of reasons why a church ought to be organized there.

4. Motion to adopt resolution as given above.

5. Names of those proposing to vote for and sign the said resolution called, and letters of dismission from other churches of like faith and order read.

6. Motion is put and if carried, the parties sign the resolution. (Before motion is put all items will be discussed and settled, such as the name, the covenant and articles of faith).

7. The permanent officers of the church are elected, provided that only those necessary at the time are to be chosen in order to avoid haste.

8. The right hand of fellowship is given to the members of the new church by the members of the council or the ministers present from other churches of like faith and order.

9. Doors of church opened to receive members in the usual way.

10. Benediction.

Officers of the Church
THE PASTOR

1. The chief officer of the church is the pastor. He is a man called of God to preach the gospel, who has first been licensed or liberated by his church to preach, who, after he has proved his gifts as a preacher, has

been ordained by his church to the ministry and who, according to Baptist custom, has been called by the church to become its pastor.

2. As has been said, the preacher ought to be called of God, or else he cannot hope to do the Lord's work well. When a brother announces to his church that he feels the call to the ministry, his church may license or liberate him so that he may be free to exercise his gifts as a minister in order that he may prove his fitness therefor. A simple motion properly made and seconded by the church conference to license the brother to preach and duly adopted by the church in conference is all that is essential to licensing a brother to preach. The clerk of the church may furnish the brother with a copy of the minutes as his credential as a licentiate.

3. It is not customary, nor is it good practice to ordain a brother to the Baptist ministry, unless he has been called by some church to act as pastor and that church formally asks for his ordination. He may be a member of the church to which he has been called as pastor, or of some other church. If he is a member of the church asking for his ordination, it is customary for that church to ask two or more neighboring churches to send their pastors to act as representatives on a council

or presbytery, called for the purpose of examining the brother as to his fitness for the Baptist ministry and if he is found fit, to ordain him to that ministry; if on the other hand the brother is a member of another church, the church to which he has been called as pastor may ask the church of which he is a member for his ordination. In this case it is customary for the church, by resolution or motion, to authorize its pastor to assemble a council or presbytery for the purpose of examining the brother as to his fitness for the Baptist ministry and, if found fit, of ordaining him to that ministry.

4. The body authorized by the church to ordain ministers may be either a council or presbytery. These two bodies are distinguished by the fact that a council is composed of both ordained ministers and laymen, while a presbytery is composed solely of ordained ministers. Either body by the authority of the church has a perfect right to ordain ministers. In the South, however, the custom of using pastors for this purpose is almost universal. That is to say, in the South men are ordained to the ministry only by other ordained ministers, who form a presbytery, under the authority of the church. But it must be remembered that while this is true in the South,

it has been good Baptist custom through the ages to ordain by councils composed of both ordained ministers and laymen. Since the church is the supreme authority in all matters pertaining to this, it is the opinion of this writer that it may ordain one of its members to the ministry by the use of a council, composed solely of laymen. But undoubtedly it is better for the church to conform to the prevailing customs, for by so doing it will relieve itself of the possibility of criticism by other churches with which it expects to cooperate in doing the broader work of the Kingdom of God. Every pastor should familiarize himself thoroughly with the customs of the Baptists in the section of the country where he lives and should conform to them without question, for so it is better both for himself and his work.

5. The pastor, who is authorized, may invite one or more other pastors or ordained Baptist ministers to join him in the formation of the presbytery. If regularly ordained ministers are not available, the pastor may associate with himself in a council one or more serious minded and regularly ordained deacons.

6. When the presbytery or council has been formed by the choice of a moderator and

clerk, the brother is examined; first, as to his Christian experience; second, as to his call to the ministry; third, as to his soundness in the doctrine; fourth, as to practice, both from the standpoint of the local work and as to co-operating with our organized work.

7. Let it be noted here that such an examination, while it has for its primary purpose the ascertaining of whether the brother is fit for the ministry or not, should not be so conducted as to frighten or intimidate the candidate, or as if the purpose is to overtake the candidate in mistakes and thus show up his weakness and ignorance; but rather the spirit of genuine brotherliness and kindness should prevail and an effort should be made to instruct and teach the candidate, as well as to discover his fitness for the ministry.

8. If the candidate is found fit in the estimation of the presbytery or council to be ordained to the ministry, a report to that effect is made to the church. Then the church by motion or resolution authorizes the presbytery or council to proceed to the formal ordination exercises.

9. Some brother is chosen to preach a sermon, the preaching of which is preceded by the usual song, prayer, and Scripture reading service. After the sermon has been preached,

the candidate is asked to kneel and some brother chosen for the purpose prays the ordination prayer; when the prayer is completed, the candidate remains on his knees while the members of the presbytery or council lay their hands on his head as a token of his full ordination to the Baptist ministry. After this formality is completed, it is customary for some brother chosen for the purpose, in proper words, to present the candidate with the Bible (each church which ordains a brother to the ministry ought to present him with a handsome and durably made copy of the Holy Scriptures, suitably inscribed). Another brother then delivers the charge to the candidate; which is followed by the charge to the church, which is delivered by still another brother chosen for the purpose. These formalities completed, the presbytery or council and the membership of the church give to the candidate the right hand of fellowship, after which he pronounces the benediction.

10. The clerk of the church should prepare a transcript of the minutes pertaining to the ordination of the candidate, which should be signed by the pastor, the clerk, and members of the presbytery or council and given to the candidate as his credentials.

THE DEACONS

1. The deacons compose that other class of officers as recognized in the New Testament. They are elected by the church from its membership—the election should be by ballot. It is preferable that no nominations be made and that the members be allowed to make their own choice without formal suggestion. The number of deacons, according to our custom, varies. The first deacons of the church in Jerusalem were seven in number, but it is not always possible to have seven, since in some small churches there is no need for them in the first place and there are not sufficient suitable men to fill the places. On the other hand, in very large churches seven deacons are not sufficient to carry the weight of the business of the church and to discharge the other obligations of the diaconate. In recent years many of those most familiar with efficient church methods urge that at least one deacon for every twenty-five members should be chosen.

2. The length of service of the deacon is not set forth in the New Testament. The general assumption and practice of Baptists until very recent times was to recognize the office of deacon as a life office; but in more recent years many churches have arranged that their deacons shall serve one, two or three year terms. In some cases they are eligible to succeed themselves; in others they are not eligible to succeed themselves under any circumstances, but must wait at least a year before they are eligible again for election. This seems to be a very good custom, for the deacon is placed on the same footing as the pastor, and serves in his position only so long as he may seem useful in it as judged by the church. However, let it be understood that once a deacon has been ordained, he is always thereafter a deacon in active service or not, unless of course he is excluded from the church or from the office for a just cause.

3. When new deacons are chosen by the church, if they have not already been ordained to the office, it is customary to ordain them. The procedure is much the same as that of the ordination of a minister. The church authorizes its pastor to assemble a council or presbytery for that purpose. This council or presbytery may be composed of ordained ministers or ordained deacons associated with the pastor and, while circumstances would rarely require such a thing in the South, it is the opinion of this writer that the church may authorize its Board of Deacons or members of it to ordain other deacons. The council or presbytery is organized by the election of a mod-

erator and clerk, though these formalities are rarely necessary since the pastor is moderator already and the church has its own clerk who may act in that capacity.

4. The examination of the deacon, though much briefer, should be along the same lines laid down for the examination of the candidate for the ministry. In some cases the Articles of Faith of the church are simply read and the thoroughgoing assent of each of the deacons to their teachings obtained.

5. Other formalities consist of a sermon on some subject pertaining to the duties and privileges of the deacon, an ordination prayer, during which the new deacons kneel, the laying on of hands by the members of the council or presbytery immediately after the prayer, the right hand of fellowship extended by the members of the council or presbytery and congregation, followed by the benediction.

6. The author has inaugurated the custom of holding an annual school for deacons following the annual election of deacons. This school is known as the Deacon's Fellowship School. For five weekday nights all the deacons meet at the church and are served with supper. After this a short speech is made by some suitable person on the duties, responsibilities, and privileges of the deacon. This is

followed by a lesson from some suitable book dealing with the deacon's duties or with the finances of the church, taught for forty-five minutes by some wideawake layman preferably. The last night after the usual program the new deacons are ordained in the approved Baptist way. After they are ordained then an informal speechmaking occasion is observed wherein the deacons have opportunity to express their hopes and plans in the new office to which they have been chosen. These schools have proved a blessing both to the deacons and to the church.

Other Officers of the Church

1. The modern Baptist church has many other officers, the clerk, the treasurer, the Sunday-school superintendent and so on. It is not the practice of the churches to choose deacons only for such offices, but undoubtedly if we followed the spirit of the teaching of the New Testament every officer of the church would be either an elder, bishop, pastor, or deacon.

2. The duties of the various other officers could be outlined here, but it is not deemed advisable by this writer, since there is so much other available literature on the subject. How-

ever, a remark or two pertaining to the duties
of the clerk seems needed.

THE CLERK—HIS DUTIES

1. The clerk is elected to his office by the
church. As in the case of all other officers,
he should be elected by ballot, without the
formality of nominations.

2. It is his duty to keep a record of all
activities and business of the church. The
custom in most churches is for the clerk to
make the briefest record possible of the business meetings or conferences of the church.
This is a very inadequate and unsatisfactory
practice. No history of a church could be
written from such records.

3. The clerk should be a man who attends
regularly the services of the church and he
should consider it his duty to make a complete, though brief minute of every meeting
of the church, giving the subject, the texts of
the sermons and addresses and prayer meeting talks of the pastor or visiting ministers
or other leaders from service to service, including in the minute the names of all who
unite themselves with the church and tokens
upon which they are received. In this manner not only the business meetings and conferences of the church are recorded in the

minutes, but each service and its outstanding features are recorded from Sunday to Sunday, Wednesday night to Wednesday night, through protracted meetings, etc.

4. One of the most important duties of the clerk is to keep a complete and up-to-the-minute roll of the church membership. He should have printed and put in a convenient place near the pulpit stand cards, upon which may be written the names and addresses of and other useful facts about those uniting with the church. As soon as an individual presents himself for membership the clerk should come forward and fill out these cards one by one. He may do this while the pastor is giving the invitation and when the invitation is completed, he may hand the cards to the pastor for use in introducing the new members to the congregation and in procuring their election to membership. Later the clerk may use the cards in completing his own records.

5. The clerk who takes an interest in his work and attempts to discharge it along the lines here suggested is a joy to his pastor and renders an incalculable service to the people of the future who will want to become acquainted with the history of the church.

6. The clerk's records should be typewritten on very strong paper and should be kept

in a looseleaf ledger style of record book. The membership roll is best kept by an index card system.

7. Every church should have a fireproof safe in which to keep all of its important documents and records, safe from fire and thief.

The Church

Its Business Session or Conference

1. It is the custom among Baptist churches to hold business sessions of the church at stated intervals, at which times all business matters of the church are discussed and provided for. These sessions are commonly called "conferences." They are held once a month and frequently on the first Wednesday or the Wednesday after the first Sunday. Some churches have found it better to arrange for the business meeting a little later in each month in order to give full time for the officials to tabulate and make a complete report of the activities of the church during the past month. The church should by all means have such a business session once a month.

2. When there is occasion for it, the moderator of the church may call the church together in extra session for the transaction of urgent business, but matters having a legal aspect should be transacted at the regular stated time for the church conference, and

churches and pastors should be careful in matters of this kind to be familiar with the state laws governing their actions and to conform to them.

3. All matters of business should be taken care of in conferences, thus leaving the other meetings of the church to be devoted entirely to worship.

4. The business session of the church is a most important one and it should not be allowed to drag or to tire the people who attend. It has come to be that most church members avoid these meetings, because they do bore the people.   A skilful pastor or moderator can so direct the business of the conference as to keep it moving in an attractive and interesting way and to bring it to a close within proper limits.   If he does, more of his people will attend and more will be interested.

5. The following order of business is a good one to follow in the conduct of business meetings:

1. Devotional.
2. Reading of the minutes.
3. Report of the clerk.
4. Report of the church treasurer.
5. Report of the Sunday school secretary.
6. Report of the Sunday school treasurer.
7. Report of other organizations, including W.M.U., B.Y.P.U's, etc., in proper order.

8. Recommendations from Board of Deacons.
9. Unfinished business and reports of committees.
10. New business.
11. Granting of church letters.
12. Invitation to church membership.
13. Song and benediction.

NOTE—The pastor or moderator should familiarize himself with the fundamental principles of parliamentary practices and should insist that the business of the church be conducted along these lines. However, he should display good sense and tact in applying these rules.

Deacons' Meeting

1. The deacons of a church should meet at least once a month at stated time for the purpose of discussing the business affairs of the church. They may also discuss any matters which concern the welfare of the church, but deacons should remember that they have no authority over the church and that they cannot take any action that is final.

2. It is well that this should be definitely understood because in not a few Baptist churches of our land the Board of Deacons is now functioning very much as the Session of a Presbyterian church, exercising the authority of the church. This is absolutely contrary to Baptist usage and principles.

3. The deacons should advise the church or recommend action to the church on any of

the matters that may come to their attention, but further than that their authority does not go. In matters of especial interest the church often instructs the deacons to act and when specifically instructed to act, they have the right to do so in the name of the church. Only under such circumstances have they such a right. However, the church cannot delegate to the Board of Deacons the right to control its affairs for a lenthy period, even if it be disposed to do so.

4. The Board of Deacons should be organized by the choice of a chairman and clerk. It is usually well for the clerk of the Board of Deacons to be the same as the clerk of the church. Sometimes the church uses the Chairman of the Board of Deacons as its moderator to preside over all the business sessions of the church. This is not a bad custom, though in most cases the pastor serves as moderator of the church.

Its Public Worship

1. It is the opinion of this writer that orderly simplicity should characterize all the services of the church. The inbred dislike by Baptists for formality, however, has led many of us into practicing very bad form in our public worship. It has come to pass that more

or less of form is desired by the churches and their constituencies for the Sunday morning service. At the same time the demand for a short service has kept pace with the other demand. This being true, the average pastor finds it difficult to keep his services within an hour or an hour and a quarter to meet the popular demands. The writer has had considerable experience at this point and has worked out the following order of worship for the morning services, which may prove helpful or suggestive to the reader:

1. Organ prelude.
2. Doxology—congregation standing.
3. Anthem—by quartet or choir.
4. Scripture reading.
5. Hymn—congregation standing.
6. Prayer.
7. Offertory—organ number.
8. Solo, duet, or other special music.
9. Sermon.
10. Invitation Hymn—congregation standing.
11. Reception of members.
12. Benediction.
13. Postlude.

2. On the other hand, the evening service, if it is made popular, while it ought to have practically all of the features of the morning service, should be informal and as far from stiffness as possible. To this end, after the

prelude there ought to be a thirty or forty-five minute period of prayer and praise or congregational singing. If a chorister may be had, it is better; if not, the pastor may lead the singing. After this period will come the offertory, an organ number, followed by special song numbers, the sermon, the invitation hymn, the benediction and the postlude.

Its Reception of Members

Strange to say, what is the proper way to receive members into the church is a question often raised. It seems that the old way is not good enough and this is the well-nigh universal experience of all pastors. Accordingly the following suggestions are made in the hope that they will prove helpful:

1. A motion and second is not essential to the reception of members. The pastor may simply ask those in favor of receiving the person offering for membership to indicate it by saying "aye" or by the uplifted hand. When this side of the question is taken, he may then let those opposed to the reception of this individual make it known by saying "no" or by the uplifted hand. In this way the embarrassment of waiting for somebody to make and some other body to second a motion is avoided. The parliamentary aspects of the

question are cared for in that all of the people are given an opportunity to express themselves either by being in favor of or as opposing the reception of the individual offering for membership.

2. Should the pastor interview those presenting themselves for baptism in the presence of the whole congregation? It may be said in this connection that the custom has been to interview such candidates concerning their Christian experience, but pastors and observers are of the opinion that such interviews are usually very unsatisfactory and not a little embarrassing to the candidate. Accordingly it is better for the interview to be held before the candidate presents him or herself for membership. But this is often impossible. Necessity for all this may be obviated by the pastor who will so state his invitation that those who accept it, in that act declare their personal faith in the Lord Jesus Christ and their desire to be baptized into the fellowship of the church. Where it is at all possible, the pastor should interview prospective candidates for baptism prior to their presenting themselves as candidates, but in every instance it is wise for the pastor so to state his invitation as that its acceptance will involve a confession of the candidate's faith in the Lord Jesus Christ and

an expression of his desire to be baptized into the full fellowship of the church.

3. When a person presents himself for membership in the church the clerk of the church should at once come forward and have the person to fill out a blank card, giving his name, residence and business addresses, telephone numbers, and other information that may be desired. These cards should be kept near the pulpit in a convenient place. They may be prepared by the pastor or clerk or both and may embrace such features as are particularly desired. When the cards are filled out they are handed to the pastor and he takes the vote as suggested above.

4. Some churches now present to each person offering for membership a card, on which is printed the Church Covenant, and he is instructed to read it carefully, because he is becoming a party to the Covenant and will be expected to live up to its provisions. Some churches even print the Covenant on the membership cards and require those offering for membership to sign the Covenant. Other pastors go further and in addition to the Covenant, propound a series of questions relating to Christian living and morals, which must be answered in the affirmative before the candidate is eligible for membership.

5. Really most of us are too lenient in the reception of members. It would be wholesome and beneficial both to church and to people if our churches were a little more exacting of the persons being received into their fellowship. Since so many churches now use the cards suggested above, forms will not be given here. Complete information about them and even the cards themselves may be procured from the publishing houses of various denominations.

Its Discipline of Its Members

Most pastors are familiar with the method and routine for the discipline of church members as outlined in the New Testament, consequently they do not need to be rehearsed here. However, one or two things need to be said.

1. Churches do not exercise discipline today as they once did; they are not strict in their requirements; their rules, if there be such, are either very lax or else very liberally interpreted.

2. There are extremes in all matters and there can be extremes in the enforcement or the lack of enforcement of the rules of the church. Every church ought to have a set of rules, formulated by itself and based on the New Testament requirements, or else ought

to recognize the New Testament requirements as its rules. If there be such rules, of course they should be enforced. If a distinction is made right here, probably such rules will come to be enforced more generally.

3. The discipline of church members must not be regarded as being wholly a matter of punishment, but should be regarded mainly as a matter of restoration. In a word, we should not seek merely to exclude members for doing what is wrong, but so to deal with them as to procure in them a recognition of the fact that they are doing wrong and a resolution on their part to discontinue this wrongdoing. This is the highest and best form of church discipline. It is undoubtedly what the Master had in mind when he suggested that the erring individual should be approached by two or three who would discuss with him his faults.

4. Great patience should be exercised by both pastor and church in matters of discipline. When committees are sent to interview those who are walking disorderly, they should be wisely chosen from among tactful and discreet men and women.

5. One of the best ways to exercise discipline is for the pastor himself to preach against the sins that are indulged in by erring members. Such preaching will accomplish much.

Very often when a church is being hurt by
numbers of its members engaging in some
frivolous and irreligious fad of the moment,
the whole matter can be rectified by holding
evangelistic services, for which the church
has been prepared by much prayer on the part
of the people and sound gospel preaching on
the part of the pastor. We hold evangelistic
meetings from year to year as a part of our
annual programs. This is well, but it should
not prevent us from holding evangelistic meetings on special occasions when our membership or a part thereof is threatened by worldli-
ness.

Its Councils

1. In latter years its councils have fallen
into disuse. Formerly they were often called
to settle most of the unfortunate disputes that
sometimes arose between factions in a church,
or between the church and its pastor. Occa-
sionally they were used to set some erring
church aright and to re-establish its standing
among other churches of the denomination.
They are discussed briefly here in the hope
that their use will be generally revived among
us, for their value cannot be questioned.

2. The Baptist Council may be composed
of three or more members of two or more

Baptist churches, or of individuals chosen
from among those who are in good standing
in the churches to which they belong. The
individuals may be pastors, or deacons, or
laymen only, or all of these.

3. The Council has no more authority than
that conferred upon it by the parties calling
for it. Baptist churches or their members
have no authority to call Councils for the
purpose of settling disputes of other Baptist
churches, unless the latter ask that such be
done.

4. When there appears to those interested
a need for a Council, it may be agreed to by
the church and called by the adoption of a
motion or resolution to that effect. Such
motion or resolution should name the churches
asked to send representatives and the number
of representatives desired from each church.
In such a case the churches named will choose
their own representatives.

5. Where a church has some disagreement
between parties of its membership, or between
certain of its members and the pastor, a Council may be agreed to by the parties to the controversy, to be composed of individuals chosen
by the two parties, without reference to their
particular church membership, except that
they must be Baptists in good standing in their

churches.   In such a case it is customary where three or more are to be chosen, for one side to choose one man, and the other side to choose one man, and the two men thus chosen to choose a third man.   The number may be increased to 5, 7, 9, or more, but the choosing must be done in the same manner as the choice of the three: each side will choose an equal number, and the number thus chosen will choose the final member of the Council.

6. Councils can be of little service unless those who are in disagreement bind themselves beforehand to be governed by the findings and decisions of the Council.   Councils called merely to give advice and which are clothed with no judicial powers are seldom of any benefit whatever.

7. When the members of the Council have come together, it is customary for them to organize by the choice of moderator and a clerk from among the number.   Then they may proceed to hear the two sides of the controversy whose merits are to be determined, to set rules governing the taking of evidence, and to establish other necessary rules of procedure.   A full and fair hearing should be accorded to all as far as possible and an unbiased judgment should be rendered.   When the Council

has completed its labors and delivered its decision it should adjourn *sine die*.

8. Once more it may be said that when disagreements arise in churches, whoever may be the parties thereto, they often could be best handled by a judicious Council after the order described above. Thus much confusion could be avoided and many reputations saved from serious impairment.

Its Ordinances

BAPTISM

1. The church has two ordinances, Baptism and the Lord's Supper. The symbolism and importance of these ordinances are fully understood. All persons professing repentance toward God and a saving faith in Jesus Christ may be received by the church as candidates for baptism.

2. The administration of the ordinance of baptism should be well and properly done, or else both its beauty and symbolism may be impaired or utterly lost. As in the case of every function or act of worship in the church, orderly simplicity should characterize it.

3. The proper administration of the ordinance may be accomplished easily, if the following simple instructions are heeded:

Where it is convenient the water in the baptistery should be warmed so that the candidate will experience no shock from cold upon entering the water. Such shocks give rise to nervousness, which later often seriously interferes with the proper administration of the ordinance, especially in the case of girls and women.

4. The candidate should be instructed to hold the knees, the back and the neck perfectly rigid, in an upright posture; to fold the hands across the breast and to yield entirely to the administrator. The minister should stand to one side of the candidate, should grasp the folded hands of the candidate in his left hand and after the formula has been said, place his right hand back of the neck of the candidate and in this fashion lower the candidate gently, very gently, into the water in such a way as to create the least commotion in the water. While the candidate is being lowered, the minister may speak reassuring words in whispers and instruct the candidate to catch his breath just before going under the water. As soon as the water has covered the candidate he may be lifted gently out of the water. When baptism is so administered the minimum of trouble is exper-

ienced and the beauty and symbolism of it are
strikingly set forth.

5. All efforts to keep the candidate from
strangling by placing a handkerchief over his
nose and mouth or by instructing the candidate to do that, should be avoided for the reason that baptism symbolizes a burial and
every act that shows the candidate as alive
operates to destroy that important feature of
its symbolism. If the candidate stands rigid
and yields himself in this rigid posture to the
minister and is gently lowered into the water
as described above, as nearly as possible, he
takes the place of a body at a burial. Also,
while we admit that the word "baptize" signi-
fies to plunge under, yet we strongly advise
ministers not to thrust their candidates under
the water, as if they were afraid they would
not get them under; and after so thrusting
them under, pull them out with equally as
much commotion, for the reason that such a
scene becomes merely a scene, without beauty
or significance, instead of displaying the symbolism intended.

6. The quotation of passages of Scripture
or poetry or other more or less spectacular
features, which are sometimes lugged into and
made part of this ordinance also should be
avoided, in that if they detract in no other

fashion, they are apt to so attract the attention of observers as to draw it from the chief thing displayed, viz., the intended symbolism of the ordinances. Again let it be said that orderly simplicity should characterize the administration of this ordinance.

7. As the ordinance of baptism is performed in different places under different circumstances, it is found necessary to adapt the administration thereof to these circumstances. Many churches are well provided with a convenient baptistery and sufficient dressing rooms. Where such is the case, of course, the administration of the ordinance may be done with more convenience and with more impressive form. On the other hand there are churches which have only a baptistery and two dressing rooms. Again, many country churches still depend upon rivers, creeks, or lakes to furnish places for baptizings. No pastor should be discouraged because of circumstances, for there is little trouble for him to adapt the forms and ceremonies which are proper and add impressiveness and beauty to the administration of baptism so as to fit the peculiar circumstances in which he finds himself. If a young pastor is in doubt about how to do these things, let him consult older and more experienced brethren.

8. The formula which has been used by the writer for twenty years is as follows:

"In obedience to the command of our Lord and Saviour Jesus Christ and upon the profession of your faith in him, I baptize you, my brother (or sister), into the name of the Father, the Son, and the Holy Spirit.   Amen."

9. A second formula is as follows:

"In obedience to the command of our Lord and Saviour Jesus Christ and upon your profession of faith in him, I baptize you, my brother (or sister), ———————————— into the name of the Father, the Son, and the Holy Spirit. Amen."

10. A third formula is as follows:

"——— ——— ———, in obedience to the command of our Lord and Saviour Jesus Christ and upon the profession of your faith in him, I baptize you, my brother (or sister), into Jesus Christ in the name of the Father, the Son, and the Holy Spirit. Amen."

11. Baptists are opposed to forms, ceremonies, and ritualism and for that reason they receive with little hospitality any suggestions that look in the direction of these. Yet everything that is done must be done in some form and in our effort to avoid form, we often succeed in doing what we attempt, in very bad form only. Therefore, the writer dares to suggest a form for the administration of the ordinance of baptism, not expecting it, nor yet intending it to be used out of the book, as

do Episcopalians and others, but only to serve
as a model, by which the pastor may fashion
his own form of doing the thing.

12. It will be observed in the form that follows that the baptizing takes place at the beginning of the service. This is as it should be,
because it gives baptism a prominent place in
the service and thereby places upon its importance the proper emphasis. It is to be
hoped that the old custom of baptizing at the
close of the service will soon cease. There are
obvious reasons for this, one of the most important being that no opportunity is provided
for giving the newly baptized the right hand
of church fellowship. Other reasons need not
be named here.

ADMINISTRATION OF THE ORDINANCE OF BAPTISM

The candidates should occupy front seats
at the opening of the service. After a song
or songs have been sung and prayer offered,
the minister may read Matthew 3: 1-17:

"And in those days cometh John the Baptist, preaching in the wilderness of Judea, saying, repent ye; for the kingdom of heaven is
at hand. For this is he that was spoken of
through Isaiah the prophet, saying, The voice
of one crying in the wilderness, make ye ready

the way of the Lord, make his paths straight. Now John himself had his raiment of camel's hair, and a leathern girdle about his loins; and his food was locusts and wild honey. Then went out unto him Jerusalem, and all Judea, and all the region round about the Jordan; and they were baptized of him in the river Jordan, confessing their sins. But when he saw many of the Pharisees and Sadducees coming to his baptism, he said unto them, ye offspring of vipers, who warned you to flee from the wrath to come? Bring forth therefore fruit worthy of repentance: and think not to say within yourselves, We have Abraham to our father: for I say unto you, that God is able of these stones to raise up children unto Abraham. And even now the axe lieth at the root of the trees; every tree therefore that bringeth not forth good fruit is hewn down, and cast into the fire. I indeed baptize you in water unto repentance; but he that cometh after me is mightier than I, whose shoes I am not worthy to bear: he shall baptize you in the Holy Spirit and in fire: whose fan is in his hand, and he will thoroughly cleanse his threshing-floor; and he will gather his wheat into the garner, but the chaff he will burn up with unquenchable fire.

Then cometh Jesus from Galilee, to the Jordan unto John, to be baptized of him. But John would have hindered him, saying, I have need to be baptized of thee, and comest thou to me? But Jesus answering said unto him, suffer it now: for thus it becometh us to fulfil all righteousness. Then he suffereth him. And Jesus, when he was baptized, went up straightway from the water: and lo, the heavens were opened unto him, and he saw the Spirit of God descending as a dove, and coming upon him; and lo, a voice out of the heavens, saying, This is my beloved Son, in whom I am well pleased."

Acts 8: 26-39: "But an angel of the Lord spake unto Philip, saying, Arise, and go toward the south unto the way that goeth down from Jerusalem unto Gaza: the same is desert. And he arose and went: and behold, a man of Ethiopia, a eunuch of great authority under Candace, queen of the Ethiopians, who was over all her treasure, who had come to Jerusalem to worship; and he was returning and sitting in his chariot, and was reading the prophet Isaiah. And the Spirit said unto Philip, Go near and join thyself to this chariot. And Philip ran to him, and heard him reading Isaiah the prophet, and said, Understandest thou what thou readest? And he said, How can I, except some one shall guide me? And he besought Philip to come up and sit with him. Now the passage of the scripture which he was reading was this, He was led as a sheep to the slaughter; and as a lamb before his shearer is dumb, so he openeth not his mouth: in his humiliation his judgment was taken away: his generation who shall declare? For his life is taken from the earth. And the eunuch answered Philip, and said, I pray thee, of whom speaketh the prophet this? of himself or of some other? And Philip opened his mouth, and beginning from this scripture, preached unto him Jesus. And as they went on the way, they came unto a certain water; and the eunuch saith, Behold, here is water; what doth hinder me to be baptized? And he commanded the chariot to stand still: and they both went down into the water, both Philip and the eunuch; and he baptized him. And when they came up out of the water, the Spirit of the Lord caught away Philip; and the eunuch saw him no more, for he went on his way rejoicing."

Then the pastor may say: we will now retire and prepare for the administration of the ordinance, and while we are so doing, the choir will sing an appropriate selection (the pastor may announce the selection himself, or may ask some brother to make some remarks upon the subject).

The pastor and the candidates then appear in the baptistery and the ordinance is administered to each in succession as described above. (The organist may render in subdued tones some suitable hymn as the ordinance is being administered to the candidates or some brother chosen for the purpose may stand just to the side of the baptistery and read a suitable verse of Scripture just before each person is baptized, thus may be read the description of Jesus' baptism as found in Mark, Luke, or John, it being read verse by verse, one verse with the baptism of each individual).

When the baptism of the candidates is completed and while the pastor and the candidates are getting ready to return to the auditorium the congregation, led by some suitable person, may engage in a prayer and praise service.

Upon the return of the pastor and the candidates to the auditorium, the candidates should be asked to occupy front seats, and as they take their places they and the pastor and the congregation should stand and the pastor should read or the pastor and the congregation and the candidates in concert should read Romans 6: 4-11:

"We were buried therefore with him through baptism into death: that like as Christ was raised from the dead through the glory of the Father, so we also might walk in newness of life. For if we have become united with him in the likeness of his death, we shall be also in the likeness of his resurrection; knowing this, that our old man was crucified with him, that the body of sin might be done away, that so we should no longer be in bondage to sin; for he that hath died is justified from sin. But if we died with Christ, we believe that we shall also live with him; knowing that Christ being raised from the dead dieth no more; death no more hath dominion over him. For the death that he died, he died unto sin once: but the life that he liveth, he liveth unto God. Even so reckon ye also yourselves to be dead unto sin, but alive unto God in Christ Jesus."

After which the congregation may be seated.

Sermon by Pastor.

Hymn.

At the conclusion of the service the candidates are given the right hand of church fellowship.

Benediction.

THE LORD'S SUPPER

1. What has been said of other features of worship in the church must be said also of the Lord's Supper. Its administration should be characterized by orderly simplicity or else its significance may be lost or at any rate impaired.

2. In most modern churches the individual cup is now used. These cups are filled and placed in a convenient tray and put on the table for use at the proper time. It often happens also that for convenience the bread is broken into small bits before it is placed upon the table. Right here care should be exercised by the pastor because much impressiveness of the service may be lost by his failure to break the bread or to pour the wine in imitation of our Lord. He should instruct those preparing the elements to leave at least one piece of bread unbroken and at the proper time he should proceed to bless and break and give the bread to the deacons in proper order; also he should instruct those preparing the elements to leave a half dozen or more cups unfilled and place the bottle or the decanter on the table and when the proper time comes he should take the receptacle and in imitation of our Lord pour the wine into the empty cups. In breaking the bread and hand-

ling the elements the pastor should exercise due care as to the cleanliness of his hands. It is better that he should instruct those preparing the elements to place at his disposal two clean napkins or a pair of clean white gloves. He may take the napkins, place them on his hands, pick up the bread and break it between the napkins, thus avoiding contact between his fingers and the bread, or he may use the gloves. The latter is better and reassures the congregation as to proper sanitary precautions.

3. If the congregation is large, there should be a sufficient number of plates and cup trays to permit a dozen or more of the deacons to wait upon the congregation at once. In this way the distribution of the bread and of the wine may be procured in brief time, as well as in an orderly manner. This is an important service and its impressiveness is by no means hindered by reasonable brevity, but rather enhanced thereby.

4. If the congregation has not been so instructed, it is the duty of the pastor to instruct those receiving the bread and wine to hold in hand these elements until every member of the congregation has been served. Then the pastor will lead the congregation in eating the bread by placing the bread in his mouth at

the proper time and likewise when the wine is served he will lead the congregation in drinking the wine at the proper time. Possibly the time will come when the receptacle will serve to carry both bread and wine and thus save double distribution.

5. The question as to the elements to be used in celebrating the Lord's Supper is often raised. Some denominations insist upon the use of fermented wine and unleavened bread. Since prohibition has prevailed in the United States most evangelical churches use the unfermented juice of the grape and since there is some question as to whether the wine of the New Testament time was fermented or not, it seems entirely proper to use the juice of the grape. Many churches are now using ordinary bread or crackers instead of the unleavened bread. It seems to the writer that unleavened bread only should be used since there is no sound reason and no question against its use, while on the other hand there is ample New Testament precedent for its use.

6. Another question is often raised and that is as to how often should the Lord's Supper be celebrated. There are some denominations of Christians which celebrate it every Lord's Day. Among Baptists the custom varies.

Some churches celebrate it the first Sunday in each month, others the first Sunday in each quarter, others semi-annually and still others but once a year. Where there is such a variety among an independent people it would be hard to procure uniformity, if such were actually desirable. The writer, in common with very many others, believes that the Lord's Supper celebrated at the end of the morning service the first Sunday in each month loses much of its impressiveness and frequently it is hastily done. It is tacked on to the end of the service and prolongs the service, so that people often avoid that particular service. It ought to be celebrated not oftener than once a quarter and then it should be given a prominent place in the service, or the whole service should be made to revolve around it. One pastor has inaugurated the scheme of celebrating the Lord's Supper just before the offertory in his services. A little thought will lead the pastor to the proper conclusion in the matter.

7. As in the case of baptism, a model form for the administration of the Lord's Supper may be found on next page.

ADMINISTRATION OF THE LORD'S SUPPER

(Preliminary exercises may be determined by the exercises of the church).

The services may be opened by song or prayer or an organ prelude, followed by these. Or this form may be observed at the conclusion of any ordinary service.

When the pastor and congregation are ready for the observance of the Lord's Supper the minister may say, Luke 22: 7-22:

"And the day of unleavened bread came, on which the passover must be sacrificed. And he sent Peter and John, saying, Go and make ready for us the passover, that we may eat. And they said unto him, Where wilt thou that we make ready? And he said unto them, Behold when ye are entered into the city, there shall meet you a man bearing a pitcher of water; follow him into the house whereinto he goeth. And ye shall say unto the master of the house, The Teacher saith unto thee, Where is the guest chamber, where I shall eat the passover with my disciples? And he will show you a large upper room furnished: there make ready. And they went, and found as he had said unto them: and they made ready the passover.

"And when the hour was come, he sat down, and the apostles with him. And he said unto them, With desire I have desired to eat this passover with you before I suffer: for I say unto you, I shall not eat it, until it be fulfilled in the kingdom of God. And he received a cup, and when he had given thanks, he said, Take this, and divide it among yourselves: for I say unto you, I shall not drink from henceforth of the fruit of the vine, until the kingdom of God shall come. And he took bread, and when he had given thanks, he brake it, and gave to them, saying, This is my body which is given for you: this do in remembrance of me. And the cup in like manner after supper, saying, This cup is the new covenant in my blood, even that which is poured out for you. But behold, the hand of him that betrayeth me is with me on the table. For the son of man indeed goeth, as it hath been determined; but woe unto the man through whom he is betrayed!"

Then the pastor may say:

We now come to observe the ordinance of the Lord's Supper, given to us to celebrate in memory of his broken body and shed blood. It is said that on the night before he was betrayed, at the conclusion of the feast of the passover which he and his disciples were celebrating, he took bread and having blessed it, brake it and gave to his disciples and said "this is my body, which is given for you."

Prayer.

(Pastor breaks the bread, hands the plates to the deacons for distribution in the congregation. The members of the congregation are expected to hold the bread in hand until all have been waited upon).

When the bread is in the hands of all, the pastor may say John 6: 58:

"This is the bread which came down out of heaven: not as the fathers ate, and died; he that eateth this bread shall live forever."

(After which he eats the bread, the members following his lead in doing the same).

Then the minister may say:

On that same night our Lord took the cup and having blessed it, gave to his disciples and said: "This is my blood which was shed for you."

Prayer.

(After the prayer the pastor pours the wine into the empty cups and hands to the deacons for distribution among the membership).

When all have been served, the pastor, taking the cup, may say:

"And according to the law, I may almost say, all things are cleansed with blood, and apart from shedding of blood there is no remission" (Hebrews 9: 22).

"But if we walk in the light, as he is in the light, we have fellowship one with another, and the blood of Jesus his Son cleanseth us from all sin" (1 John 1: 7).

(After this he leads the congregation in drinking the wine).

Then the pastor may say:

"For as often as ye eat this bread, and drink the cup, ye proclaim the Lord's death till he come" (1 Cor. 11: 26).

Then the pastor may say:

After our Lord and his disciples ate the bread and drank the wine, celebrating thus the first Supper of our Lord, it is said that they sang a hymn and went out. Let us now sing and as we sing, we will follow the age-old custom of making an offering for the poor. Accordingly the deacons will pass through the audience, taking the collection. This will conclude the service.

Administration of the Ordinances of Baptism and the Lord's Supper and the Induction of Newly Made Christians into the Full Privileges and Responsibilities of Church Membership

1. In view of the fact that many of our churches in celebrating the ordinances have come to do so in a manner which is calculated to subtract impressiveness therefrom, the writer has originated the following form wherein both ordinances are celebrated conjointly in one service and the newly baptized members are formally inducted into the full fellowship of the church.

2. The model for this service follows and has been used often enough to prove its merit and propriety. Pastors are hereby requested to use it at least once at the conclusion of evangelistic meetings. So far it has never failed to be a high tide service. Both ordinances are made to stand out and both of them impress themselves upon the candidates bap-

tized and received into the church on that occasion in a way that the candidates can never forget.

3. This service can be put on in any church, even though it be a country church where the baptizing is performed in a creek or river or other body of water. The preliminary exercises as outlined below in such a case may be held on the banks of the body of water and when the baptismal services are completed all may return to the church, where the rest of the services may be observed.

This form, as other forms in the book, is but a model and is given to suggest other models of a like nature. It may be used or not, just as the pastor may determine.

(Preliminary exercises may be determined by the circumstances of the church).

The services may be opened by songs and prayer or by an organ prelude, followed by songs and prayer.

At the opening of the service the candidates for baptism occupy front seats and when the opening songs have been sung and prayers offered, the pastor may read Matthew 3: 1-17:

"And in those days cometh John the Baptist, preaching in the wilderness of Judea, saying, Repent ye, for the kingdom of heaven is at hand. For this is he that was spoken of through Isaiah the prophet, saying, The voice of one crying in the wilderness, make ye ready the way of the Lord, make his paths straight. Now John himself had his raiment of camel's hair, and a leathern girdle about his loins; and his food was locusts and wild honey. Then went out unto him Jerusalem, and all Judea, and all the region round about the Jordan; and they were baptized of him in the river Jordan, confessing their sins. But when he saw many of the Pharisees and Sadducees coming to his baptism, he said unto them, Ye offspring of vipers, who warned you to flee from the wrath to come? Bring forth therefore fruit worthy of repentance: and think not to say within yourselves, We have Abraham to our father: for I say unto you, that God is able of these stones to raise up children unto Abraham. And even now the axe lieth at the root of the trees: every tree therefore that bringeth not forth good fruit is hewn down, and cast into the fire. I indeed baptize you in water unto repentance: but he that cometh after me is mightier than I, whose shoes I am not worthy to bear: he shall baptize you in the Holy Spirit and in fire: whose fan is in his hand, and he will thoroughly cleanse his threshing-floor; and he will gather his wheat into the garner, but the chaff he will burn up with unquenchable fire.

Then cometh Jesus from Galilee to the Jordan unto John, to be baptized of him. But John would have hindered him, saying, I have need to be baptized of thee, and comest thou to me? But Jesus answering said unto him, Suffer it now: for thus it becometh us to fulfil all righteousness. Then he suffereth him. And Jesus, when he was baptized, went up straightway from the water: and lo, the heavens were opened unto him, and he saw the Spirit of God descending as a dove, and coming upon him; and lo, a voice out of the heavens, saying, This is my beloved son, in whom I am well pleased."

Acts 8: 26-39: "But an angel of the Lord spake unto Philip, saying, Arise, and go toward the south unto the way that goeth down from Jerusalem unto Gaza: the same is desert. And he arose and went: and behold a man of Ethiopia, a eunuch of great authority under Candace, queen of the Ethiopians, who was over all her treasure, who had come to Jerusalem to worship; and he was returning and sitting in his chariot, and was reading the prophet Isaiah. And the Spirit said unto Philip, Go near and join thyself to this chariot. And Philip ran to him, and heard him reading Isaiah the prophet, and said, Understandeth thou what thou readest? And he said, How can I, except some one shall guide me? And he besought Philip to come up and sit with him. Now the passage of the scripture which he was reading was this, He was led as a sheep to the slaughter; and as a lamb before his shearer is dumb, so he openeth not his mouth: in his humiliation his judgment was taken away: his generation who shall declare? For his life is taken from the earth. And the eunuch answered Philip, and said, I pray thee, of whom speaketh the prophet this? of himself, or of some other?   And Philip opened his mouth and beginning from this scripture, preached unto him Jesus. And as they went on the way, they came unto a certain water; and the eunuch saith, Behold, here is water; what doth hinder me to be baptized? And he commanded the chariot to stand still: and they both went down into the water, both Philip and the eunuch; and he baptized him. And when they came up out of the water, the Spirit of the Lord caught away Philip; and the eunuch saw him no more, for he went on his way rejoicing."

Then the pastor may say:

The following brethren and sisters————
————————, having been duly received by

this church as candidates for baptism, are now to be baptized.

While the congregation sings a suitable hymn (pastor may announce hymn or instead may invite some brother to make remarks upon the subject of baptism) the pastor and candidates will retire and prepare for the ordinance.

Then the candidates are baptized one by one.

(While the ordinance is being administered the organist may play in subdued tones some old, suitable hymn, or the pastor may instruct some brother to read suitable passages of scripture, verse by verse).

When the ordinance has been completed, the congregation may engage in a prayer and praise service, awaiting the return of the pastor and the newly baptized members to the auditorium.

Upon the return of the pastor and those newly baptized to the auditorium the congregation will stand. (The pastor will occupy his place on the pulpit stand and the newly baptized members will occupy front seats). Then the pastor, or the pastor and congregation in unison, or the pastor and congregation in concert, may read Romans 6: 4-11:

"We were buried therefore with him through baptism into death: that like as Christ

was raised from the dead through the glory
of the Father, so we also might walk in newness of life.   For if we have become united
with him in the likeness of his death, we shall
be also in the likeness of his resurrection;
knowing this that our old man was crucified
with him, that the body of sin might be done
away, that so we should no longer be in bondage to sin; for he that hath died is justified
from sin.   But if we died with Christ, we believe that we shall also live with him; knowing
that Christ being raised from the dead dieth
no more; death no more hath dominion over
him.   For the death that he died, he died unto
sin once: but the life that he liveth, he liveth
unto God.   Even so reckon ye also yourselves
to be dead unto sin, but alive unto God in
Christ Jesus."

Sermon: (on the subject of the ordinances, and
the privileges, duties, and responsibilities of church
membership).

After the sermon has been completed, the
pastor may take his place at the Lord's table
and read Luke 22: 7-22:

"And the day of unleavened bread came,
on which the passover must be sacrificed.   And
he sent Peter and John, saying, Go and make
ready for us the passover, that we may eat.
And they said unto him, Where wilt thou that

we make ready? And he said unto them, Behold when ye are entered into the city, there shall meet you a man bearing a pitcher of water; follow him into the house whereinto he goeth. And ye shall say unto the master of the house, The Teacher saith unto thee, where is the guest chamber, where I shall eat the passover with my disciples? And he will show you a large upper room furnished: there make ready. And they went, and found as he had said unto them: and they made ready the passover.

"And when the hour was come, he sat down and the apostles with him. And he said unto them, With desire I have desired to eat this passover with you before I suffer: for I say unto you, I shall not eat it, until it be fulfilled in the kingdom of God. And he received a cup, and when he had given thanks, he said, Take this, and divide it among yourselves: for I say unto you, I shall not drink from henceforth of the fruit of the vine, until the kingdom of God shall come. And he took bread, and when he had given thanks, he brake it, and gave to them, saying, This is my body which is given for you: this do in remembrance of me. And the cup in like manner after supper, saying, This cup is the new covenant in my blood, even that which is poured out for you.

But behold, the hand of him that betrayeth me is with me on the table. For the son of man indeed goeth, as it hath been determined: but woe unto that man through whom he is betrayed!"

Then the pastor may say:

Having seen the ordinance of baptism administered in this service, we now come to observe that other ordinance of the church, the Supper of our Lord, given to us to celebrate in memory of his broken body and shed blood. It is said that on the night before he was betrayed, at the conclusion of the feast of the passover which he and his disciples were celebrating, he took bread and having blessed it, brake it and gave to his disciples and said "this is my body, which is given for you."

Prayer.

(Pastor breaks the bread, hands the plates to the deacons for distribution in the congregation. The members of the congregation are expected to hold the bread in hand until all have been waited upon).

When the bread is in the hands of all, the pastor may say, John 6: 58:

"This is the bread which came down out of heaven: not as the fathers ate, and died; he that eateth this bread, shall live for ever."

(After which he eats the bread, the members following his lead, doing the same).

Then the minister may say:

On that same night our Lord took the cup and having blessed it, gave to his disciples and said: "This is my blood of the covenant, which is poured out for many unto the remission of sins."

Prayer.

(After the prayer the pastor pours the wine into the empty cups and hands to the deacons for distribution among the membership).

When all have been served, the pastor, taking the cup, may say, Hebrews 9: 22:

"According to the law, I may almost say, all things are cleansed with blood, and apart from shedding of blood there is no remission."

1 John 1: 7: "But if we walk in the light, as he is in the light, we have fellowship one with another, and the blood of Jesus his Son cleanseth us from all sin."

(After this he leads the congregation in drinking the wine).

Then the pastor may say, 1 Cor. 11: 26:

"For as often as ye eat this bread, and drink the cup, ye proclaim the Lord's death till he come."

Then the pastor may say:

After our Lord and his disciples ate the bread and drank the wine, it is said that they sang a hymn and went out. We will now sing a hymn and while it is being sung we will give the right hand of full church fellowship to the newly baptized members, which act will conclude the services of the hour.

Notes on Laying Corner Stone for Church Building

1. The meeting should have a presiding officer, preferably known as moderator, since presiding officers among Baptists are generally called moderators. The pastor, the chairman of the Board of Deacons, or some other individual may be chosen for the place.

2. There should also be some person designated to place the mementos in the stone or metal receptacle. The clerk of the church or some other specially designated person may perform the service.

3. The corner stone should be suspended or handily placed so that it can be put in position with greatest ease.

4. A roll of the church members, a Bible, copies of current association and state convention minutes, resolutions pertaining to the erection of the building as adopted by the church, newspapers containing accounts of the church and its work and a brief history thereof specially prepared, should be placed

in the receptacle, together with such other special articles as may seem desirable. The clerk should call these items out, one by one, as they are placed in the receptacle.

5. A suitable sermon or address should be delivered by some speaker chosen for the purpose. The moderator and the speaker should not be the same person.

6. The following model form was originated by the writer because of the demand for such a form. Being often approached by brethren, asking information how to do this one thing and having to perform the service without aid on numerous occasions, the writer prepared this form and hereby submits it for consideration of those interested.

7. The pastor may sometimes find himself called upon to take part in laying a cornerstone in connection with some order, such as the Masons. When he is called upon to do such a thing, he should have an understanding with the parties having in charge the ceremonies performed by the order in question and should have a definite agreement as to just what part he shall take and when. A little consulation between the pastor and the head of the order will make it easy for the ceremonies to be so arranged as to give all parties some proper place in the ceremonies.

Laying a Church Corner Stone

Doxology.

Invocation.

Moderator reads Acts 17: 22-31:

"And Paul stood in the midst of the Areopagus, and said, Ye men of Athens, in all things I perceive that ye are very religious. For as I passed along, and observed the objects of your worship, I found also an altar with this inscription, TO AN UNKNOWN GOD. What therefore ye worship in ignorance, this I set forth unto you. The God that made the world, and all things therein, he, being Lord of heaven and earth, dwelleth not in temples made with hands; neither is he served by men's hands, as though he needed anything, seeing he himself giveth to all life, and breath, and all things; and he made of one every nation of men to dwell on all the face of the earth, having determined their appointed seasons, and the bounds of their habitation; that they should seek God, if haply they might feel after him and find him, though he is not far from each one of us: for in him we live, and move, and have our being; as certain even of your own poets have said, For we are also his offspring. Being then the offspring of God, we ought not to think that the Godhead is like unto gold, or silver, or stone, graven by art and device of man. The times of ignorance therefore God overlooked; but now he commandeth men that they should all everywhere repent: inasmuch as he hath appointed a day in which he will judge the world in righteousness by the man whom he hath ordained; whereof he hath given assurance unto all men, in that he hath raised him from the dead."

Hymn: "My Hope Is Built On Nothing Less."

Moderator again reads:

Psalm 127: 1: "Except Jehovah build the house, they labor in vain that build it: except Jehovah keep the city, the watchman waketh but in vain."

1 Cor. 3: 10-15: "According to the grace of God which was given unto me, as a wise master builder I laid a foundation; and another buildeth thereon. But let each man take heed how he buildeth thereon. For other foundation can no man lay than that which is

laid, which is Jesus Christ. But if any man buildeth on the foundation gold, silver, costly stones, wood, hay, stubble; each man's work shall be made manifest: for the day shall declare it, because it is revealed in fire; and the fire itself shall prove each man's work of what sort it is. If any man's work shall abide which he built thereon, he shall receive a reward. If any man's work shall be burned, he shall suffer loss: but he himself shall be saved; yet so as through fire."

1 Pet. 2: 6-10: "Because it is contained in scripture, Behold, I lay in Zion a chief corner stone, elect, precious: and he that believeth on him shall not be put to shame. For you therefore that believe in the preciousness: but for such as disbelieve, the stone which the builders rejected, the same was made the head of the corner; and, a stone of stumbling, and a rock of offense; for they stumble at the word, being disobedient: whereunto also they were appointed. But ye are an elect race, a royal priesthood, a holy nation, a people for God's own possession, that ye may show forth the excellencies of him who called you out of darkness into his marvelous light: who in time past were no people, but now are the people of God: who had not obtained mercy, but now have obtained mercy."

Ephes. 2: 19-22: "So then ye are no more strangers and sojourners, but ye are fellow citizens with the saints, and of the household of God, being built upon the foundation of the apostles and prophets, Christ Jesus himself being the chief corner stone; in whom each several building, fitly framed together, growing into a holy temple in the Lord; in whom ye also are builded together for a habitation of God in the Spirit."

Clerk places mementos in the receptacle.

Prayer—(By someone chosen for the purpose).

Hymn—"How Firm a Foundation."

Address or sermon.

Moderator (with what assistance is needed) places the stone or calls on another previously designated to perform the service, using the following formula:

"As our Lord Jesus Christ is the chief corner stone of our salvation and liberty, as the Holy Spirit hath revealed him to us, and as God the Father in love hath conceived and promulgated the whole glorious scheme of human redemption, I, therefore, lay the corner stone of the meeting house of the ———— Baptist Church in the name of the Father, the Son, and the Holy Spirit. Amen."

The moderator then addresses the audience, saying:

"Take heed therefore that the corner stone of your faith shall ever be Jesus Christ, the Son of God and our Saviour."

Hymn—"Rock of Ages."

Benediction.

Dedicating a House of Worship

(The regular standard service of the church may be used in opening. Where circumstances may so dictate, the pastor or minister in charge may alter the services to suit).

Prelude.

Invocation.

Anthem.

Then the minister may say:

"I was glad when they said unto me, Let us go unto the house of Jehovah. Our feet are standing within thy gates, O Jerusalem, Jerusalem, that art builded as a city that is compact together; whither the tribes go up, even the tribes of Jehovah, for an ordinance for Israel, to give thanks unto the name of Jehovah. For there are set thrones for judgment, the thrones of the house of David. Pray for the peace of Jerusalem: They shall prosper that love thee. Peace be within thy walls, and prosperity within thy palaces. For my brethren and companions' sakes, I will now say, peace be within thee. For the sake of the house of Jehovah our God I will seek thy good" (Psalm 122: 1-9).

Hymn—"I Love Thy Kingdom Lord" (or some other suitable selection).

Scripture Reading.

2 Chron. 6: 1, 2, 4, 14, 17-20, 39-41: "Then spake Solomon, Jehovah hath said that he would dwell in the thick darkness. But I have built thee a house of habitation, and a place for thee to dwell in for ever. . . . And he said, Blessed be Jehovah, the God of Israel, who spake with his mouth unto David my father, and hath with his hands fulfilled it. . . . and he said, O Jehovah, the God of Israel, there is no God like thee, in heaven, or on earth; who keepest covenant and loving-kindness with thy servants, that walk before thee with all their heart. . . . Now therefore, O Jehovah, the God of Israel, let thy word be verified, which thou spakest unto thy servant David. But will God in very deed dwell with men on the earth? behold, heaven and the heaven of heavens cannot contain thee; how much less this house which I have builded! Yet have thou respect unto the prayer of thy servant, and to his supplication, O Jehovah

my God, to hearken unto the cry and to the
prayer which thy servant prayeth before thee;
that thine eyes may be open toward this house
day and night, even toward the place whereof
thou hast said that thou wouldest put thy name
there; to hearken unto the prayer which thy
servant shall pray toward this place. . . .
Then hear thou from heaven, even from thy
dwelling-place, their prayer and their suppli-
cations, and maintain their cause, and forgive
thy people who have sinned against thee. Now,
O my God, let, I beseech thee, thine eyes be
open, and let thine ears be attent, unto the
prayer that is made in this place. Now therefore arise, O Jehovah God, into thy resting-
place, thou, and the ark of thy strength: let
thy priests, O Jehovah God, be clothed with
salvation, and let thy saints rejoice in goodness."

Psalm 84: 1-12: "How amiable are thy
tabernacles, O Jehovah of hosts! My soul
longeth, yea, even fainteth for the courts of Jehovah; my heart and my flesh cry out unto the
living God. Yea, the sparrow hath found her a
house, and the swallow a nest for herself,
where she may lay her young, even thine
altars, O Jehovah of hosts, my king and my
God. Blessed are they that dwell in thy house;
they will be still praising thee. (Selah)

Blessed is the man whose strength is in thee; in whose heart are the highways to Zion. Passing through the valley of weeping they make it a place of springs; yea, the early rain covereth it with blessings. They go from strength to strength; every one of them appeareth before God in Zion. O Jehovah God of hosts, hear my prayer; Give ear, O God of Jacob. (Selah) Behold, O God our shield, and look upon the face of thine anointed. For a day in thy courts is better than a thousand. I had rather be a doorkeeper in the house of my God, than to dwell in the tents of wickedness. For Jehovah God is a sun and a shield: Jehovah will give grace and glory; no good thing will he withhold from them that walk uprightly. O Jehovah of hosts, blessed is the man that trusteth in thee."

Psalm 48: 9-14: "We have thought on thy lovingkindness, O God, in the midst of thy temple. As is thy name, O God, so is thy praise unto the ends of the earth: thy right hand is full of righteousness. Let mount Zion be glad, let the daughters of Judah rejoice, because of thy judgments. Walk about Zion, and go round about her; number the towers thereof; mark ye well her bulwarks; consider her palaces: that ye may tell it to the generation following. For this God is our God for

ever and ever: He will be our guide even
unto death."

Prayer of Thanksgiving.

Offertory—(If a special offering is to be made
for the purpose of defraying some remaining in-
debtedness on the church building, the pastor may
say):

2 Cor. 9: 6-15: "But this I say, he that
soweth sparingly shall reap also sparingly;
and he that soweth bountifully shall reap also
bountifully. Let each man do according as
he hath purposed in his heart: not grudgingly,
or of necessity: for God loveth a cheerful
giver. And God is able to make all grace
abound unto you; that ye, having always all
sufficiency in everything, may abound unto
every good work: as it is written, He hath scattered abroad, he hath given to the poor; his
righteousness abideth for ever. And he that
supplieth seed to the sower and bread for
food, shall supply and multiply your seed for
sowing, and increase the fruits of your righteousness: ye being enriched in every thing
unto all liberality, which worketh through us
thanksgiving to God. For the ministration of
this service not only filleth up the measures of
the wants of the saints, but aboundeth also
through many thanksgivings unto God; seeing

that through the proving of you by this ministration they glorify God for the obedience of
your confession unto the gospel of Christ, and
for the liberality of your contribution unto
them and unto all; while they themselves also,
with supplication on your behalf, long after
you by reason of the exceeding grace of God
in you.   Thanks be to God for his unspeakable
gift."

**Then the pastor or other minister appointed to
take special offering may proceed.**

(In case only the ordinary offering of the regular service is to be taken, the minister may say):
2 Cor. 9: 6, 7: "But this I say, he that
soweth sparingly shall reap also sparingly;
and he that soweth bountifully shall reap also
bountifully.   Let each man do according as he
hath purposed in his heart: not grudgingly, or
of necessity: for God loveth a cheerful giver."

Then the minister may announce the offering.

Hymn or special selection.

Sermon or Address.

Dedicatory Prayer—(Before offering the prayer
himself or calling upon the brother chosen for the
purpose, the minister may say):

Psalm 27: 4 and 5: "One thing have I
asked of Jehovah, that will I seek after: that I

may dwell in the house of Jehovah all the days of my life, to behold the beauty of Jehovah, and to inquire in his temple. For in the day of trouble he will keep me secretly in his pavilion: in the covert of his tabernacle will he hide me; he will lift me up upon a rock."

Hymn.

Benediction.

Postlude.